# Chicken Soup for the Ocean Lover's Soul

# CHICKEN SOUP
# FOR THE
# OCEAN LOVER'S
# SOUL

## Amazing Sea Stories and Wyland Artwork to Open the Heart and Rekindle the Spirit

Jack Canfield
Mark Victor Hansen
Wyland
with Steve Creech

Health Communications, Inc.
Deerfield Beach, Florida

*www.hcibooks.com*
*www.chickensoup.com*

We would like to acknowledge the many publishers and individuals who granted us permission to reprint the cited material. (Note: The stories that were penned anonymously, that are in the public domain or that were written by Jack Canfield, Mark Victor Hansen or Wyland are not included in this listing.)

*Raising Cecily.* Reprinted by permission of Nan Lincoln. ©1986 Nan Lincoln. From *The Bar Harbor Times*, Issue: June, 1987.

*Surrogate Mom and Pup.* Reprinted by permission of Roxayne Spruance and Michelle Staedler. ©2001 Roxayne Spruance and Michelle Staedler.

*Hooked on Mahogany* and *Octopus Odyssey.* Reprinted by permission of Mike Lipstock. ©1997, 1996 Mike Lipstock.

*The Blind Diver.* Reprinted by permission of Joycebelle Edelbrock. ©2001 Joycebelle Edelbrock.

*In Harmony.* Reprinted by permission of Martha Gusukuma-Donnenfield. ©1996 Martha Gusukuma-Donnenfield. With acknowlegement to Bob Krause for the personal connection he shared with Martha's father in his final days.

*(Continued on page 292)*

**Library of Congress Cataloging-in-Publication Data**

Chicken soup for the ocean lover's soul : amazing sea stories and Wyland artwork
   to open the heart and rekindle the spirit / [compiled by] Jack Canfield,
   Mark Victor Hansen, Wyland.
      p. cm.
   ISBN 0-7573-0059-6 (tp)
      1. Marine animals—Anecdotes. 2. Human-animal relationships—Anecdotes.
   3. Ocean—Psychological aspects. I. Canfield, Jack date. II. Hansen, Mark Victor.
   III. Wyland, date.

QL121.C45 2003
508.3162—dc21

                                                                                    2003051125

Publisher: Health Communications, Inc.
         3201 S.W. 15th Street
         Deerfield Beach, FL 33442-8190

*Original paintings on cover and insides by Wyland ©2003*
*Cover design by Larissa Hise Henoch*
*Inside formatting by Dawn Von Strolley Grove*

We dedicate this book
to ocean lovers everywhere . . .

To our parents who taught us lessons of life among
the beaches, tide pools and rolling waves . . .

To the scientists who have guided us . . .

And, finally, to the writers, poets and
artists who remind us that as much
as we know, the sea will always remain,
first and foremost, a place of
infinite beauty and mystery.

*Warm Tropical Paradise*

# Contents

## 1. LIVING IN HARMONY

## 2. THE POWER TO HEAL

## 3. CELEBRATING THE BOND

## 4. OCEAN WISDOM

## 5. FRONTIERS OF THE SEA

## 6. SAILING SPIRITS

## 7. ON COURAGE AND ADVENTURE

## 8. SAVING THE SEA

# Acknowledgments

This book would never have come to be without the input of thousands of ocean lovers from as far away as New Zealand, Ireland, Iceland, Mexico, Norway, Canada, England, South Africa, Germany and Australia. It seemed as we were developing this book that ocean lovers knew neither political nor geographic boundaries, not even in the heartland of America, and flooded us with marvelous stories of experiences with sea life and family seaside vacations.

But beyond those who submitted such incredible stories, there are many, many more people to be thanked, without whom the completion of *Chicken Soup for the Ocean Lover's Soul* would never have occurred.

To Jacques Cousteau, who inspired the career of Wyland and a whole generation of people to care about ocean conservation.

To ocean icons like Dr. Sylvia Earle, Dr. Bob Ballard, Dr. Roger Payne, Lloyd Bridges, Sir Peter Blake, Bob Hunter and many others who have dedicated their lives to preserving the world's oceans. They are certainly among the more visible advocates for ocean awareness, but many more conservation organizations support them. We hope you will lend your support by giving generously to their campaigns.

We would like to thank the Wyland Foundation for bridging the worlds of art and science, and working with the Scripps Institution of Oceanography and the Birch Aquarium on a world-class, clean-water curriculum to be presented to 60 million students in the coming year. To the board of directors of the Wyland Foundation for ten great years and the many Wyland Foundation members who give unselfishly of their time and energy to help with its programs.

Wyland would like to personally express his great debt to the many scientists who have worked with him over the years, instilling in him a passion for sharing his message of ocean conservation and art with the world.

To Mark Victor Hansen, Jack Canfield, Peter Vegso and the entire family at Chicken Soup for the Soul Enterprises and Health Communications (HCI). These two fine organizations are to be truly commended for giving such a beautiful gift to the world as the series of *Chicken Soup for the Soul* books.

Big thanks to Angela Needham for spearheading this project from the very beginning. Even after six years, Angela always had the faith to see this project completed.

To Steve Creech, Wyland's cowriter and publicist, who shaped and formed the book with the support of the dedicated staff at Wyland World Headquarters. Steve's adventures collecting stories took him as far away as Valdez, Alaska.

To the entire Wyland family: Wyland's parents, Darlene and Robert, and his brothers, Steve, Bill and Tom.

To Darcy Pinon, Julie Edwards and Liz Zuercher—each gave extensive amounts of their personal time to assist with editing, compiling and rereading stories.

Thanks to Virginia Lenac for her tireless support and efforts. Virginia always went the extra mile, always with a smile, to keep this book organized and on track.

To the entire Wyland design team, including Jonathan

Dupree, Gregg Hamby, Nicole Hill, Karla Kipp, Kathy Gordon and Gino Beltran. They deserve a special nod of appreciation for ensuring that the look and feel of this book met the high standards of Chicken Soup for the Soul Enterprises and HCI.

To Julie Guerrini, who read and read and read, providing valuable insight about many of the stories in this book while never complaining, even when yet another batch of stories was given to her "just to check out."

Thanks to all the people who evaluated, commented upon and helped us improve our story selection. The panel of readers included: Sheri Arnett, Suzanne Beukema, Marie Clark, Grace Compton, Janet Creech, Robin Davis, Terrie Druehl, Sherry Eaton, Janice Glenn, Dana and Jerry Gonzales, Alice Jensen, David Norcross, Barbara O'Neill, Jennifer Paul, Sue Paul, Jennifer Scardino, Stan Stern and Lisa Trampe.

To Leslie Riskin, Kathy Brennan-Thompson, D'ette Corona, Tasha Boucher, Maria Nickless and Heather McNamara at Chicken Soup for the Soul Enterprises. What an amazing group of people! They were instrumental in walking us through the strange, unpredictable world of book publishing and took the time to help us achieve the highest level of professionalism.

To the drive of Jack Canfield and Patty Aubery to push this book through to its completion.

And, of course, thank you to the folks at HCI, including Lisa Drucker, Susan Heim and the entire team of editors, publicist Kim Weiss, and the terrific sales teams headed by Terry Burke and Tom Sand.

We would also like to acknowledge and express our appreciation to the authors of the more than 3,000 stories that we received to make this book possible.

And, last but not least, we would like to thank *you* for purchasing *Chicken Soup for the Ocean Lover's Soul*. It has been a labor of love, more than six years in the making as we've searched the planet to find stories that touch the heart and ignite the ever-growing passion for preservation of our oceans and the wonderful life within. Best fishes!

# Introduction

All of us, at one time or another, find ourselves drawn to the sea. For some, it's a place for reflection or romance. For others, it's the thrill of watching surf crash against a sandy white beach or studying the kaleidoscope of life among a tropical coral reef. This ability of the ocean to change our lives, to inspire and fascinate us, is what led us to create *Chicken Soup for the Ocean Lover's Soul,* a collection of stories from around the world that celebrate the magic of our ocean planet.

I first embraced the ocean on a family vacation to Southern California many years ago. I was only fourteen years old and experiencing the cool waters of the Pacific for the first time. Amazingly, as I looked out across the endless expanse, lost in its sheer size, two fifty-foot gray whales broke the surface and spouted right before my eyes.

After that encounter I dedicated myself to the preservation of these gentle giants and the oceans they needed for survival. I truly believe that when you see a whale you become a better human being. Over the years, I have talked with many people who have told me of encounters with marine mammals, and they all have experienced similar transformations.

I had the honor of meeting Mark Victor Hansen at one of my gallery shows in Kona on the big island of Hawaii. We connected immediately as I felt Mark's commitment with Jack Canfield not only to create a fantastic book filled with wonderful stories of the ocean, but also their commitment to the conservation of this precious resource. As we continued to discuss the possibility of creating this unique book, it became clear to us that the oceans have been the source of many inspirational stories over the years.

Now, after diving with these two ocean lovers, we are ready to share these uplifting, engaging and, above all, true stories from people such as renowned wildlife expert and television personality Jack Hanna, ocean researcher Dr. Sylvia Earle, writer Clive Cussler and many others. This beautiful book and the series of marine life paintings it contains reflect the rare beauty of the sea for the ocean lover's soul.

A portion of all proceeds from *Chicken Soup for the Ocean Lover's Soul* will go the Wyland Foundation, which has partnered with the Scripps Institution of Oceanography at the University of California, San Diego, to create a free, nationwide marine life art and science educational program for every school in the nation. This program is designed to teach children everywhere about the importance of our marine resources. Your purchase of this book will help make this program a great success.

Best fishes and aloha,
*Wyland*

# Share with Us

We would love to hear your reactions to the stories in this book. Please let us know what your favorite stories were and how they affected you.

We also invite you to send us stories you would like to see published in future editions of *Chicken Soup for the Soul*. Please send submissions to:

*Chicken Soup for the Soul*
P.O. Box 30880
Santa Barbara, CA 93130
fax: 805-563-2945

You can also visit or access e-mail at the *Chicken Soup for the Soul* site:

*www.chickensoup.com*

We hope you enjoy reading this book as much as we enjoyed compiling, editing and writing it.

# 1

# LIVING IN HARMONY

*A*ll good things are wild and free.

Henry David Thoreau

# Raising Cecily

*Until one has loved an animal, a part of one's
soul remains unawakened.*

Anatole France

On a chilly, gray morning in late May, the insistent ringing of the phone brought me dashing up from the garden.
It was Bob, my husband, who was working on a summer
cottage near our home on Mount Desert Island, Maine.

"Nan, get the kids and come over here," he said. "There's
something you should see."

Glad for the excuse to escape the blackflies, I loaded
the kids into the car and drove the short distance to the
cottage.

The "something" turned out to be a harbor seal pup—a
forlorn and furry little bundle huddled against a large rock
at the high-tide line. My first instinct was to offer immedi-
ate aid and comfort to the frightened creature, as one would
any lost baby, but I knew better and resisted the urge.

Most seal pups that people find "abandoned" on reefs,
rocks and beaches are not abandoned at all; they are
merely waiting for their mothers to return from fishing.

Although it is unusual for their mothers to leave them on a mainland beach, it isn't unheard-of.

Bob and I decided to call the Department of Wildlife to ask what we should do. The local game warden told us to wait for a complete tide change—about six hours—to see if the pup's mother returned. With no sighting of the mother, we called Steve Katona, director of Allied Whale, a marine research program at College of the Atlantic in nearby Bar Harbor. Steve gave us permission to foster the pup ourselves, under his supervision, until it was healthy enough to be returned to the wild.

We wrapped the shivering little pup, whom we had already named Cecily, into a wool blanket and carried her home. After laying her down on a tarp in the spare bedroom, I went to prepare the formula Steve had dictated to me—a rich concoction of cream, egg yolks, fish oil and baby vitamins. Steve had warned me that few abandoned seal pups survive—either because they are sickly to begin with or because they refuse to nurse from a bottle designed for human babies. Eager to help the starving pup, I never even considered failure.

But three hours later, with both of us reeking of fish oil and cream and crying—Cecily with hunger and I with frustration—I had to concede I was losing this life-and-death struggle. Although Cecily sucked hungrily on my arms, legs and fingers when I poured the formula on them, she refused to have anything to do with the rubber nipple on the bottle.

In a last attempt, I removed the offending nipple and replaced it with a triangular piece of sponge. Then tucking the bottle into the crook of my elbow with the sponge barely protruding from the other side, I squeezed a steady stream of formula down the outside of my arm. Cecily lapped at the formula, nuzzling closer and closer to the hidden sponge nipple. Finally, she latched onto the sponge and drained the bottle. Then, with considerable gusto, she finished a second one.

Weak-kneed and shaking, I stumbled upstairs to say goodnight to my children. As I leaned over to kiss my son, he wrinkled his nose and told me I smelled like fish bait. "That," I told him, "is the sweet smell of victory." It was a smell that grew quickly familiar. Every four hours from then on, Cecily would announce her hunger with loud whoops from the spare bedroom.

Cecily gained weight rapidly in the days that followed. Her body, which had resembled a stuffed toy with half the stuffing missing, had filled out like a fat little blimp, and her dark, dappled fur grew thick and glossy.

She had bonded with me completely after that first feeding, just as she would have with her own mother. She tolerated occasional pats from Bob and the kids, but most of her waking hours were spent at my feet with one flipper wrapped around my ankle. She even terrorized our seventy-five-pound malamute and our cat with warning snorts and sneezes whenever either of them dared approach "mom territory."

Cecily had gained about ten pounds in less than a week on the fat-rich formula, and Steve Katona suggested I try her out in the ocean. Although I realized swimming was a necessary part of her education, I dreaded the moment. I was worried that as soon as she tasted the salty water and felt the compelling currents wash against her flippers, she would disappear, like a bird from a cage, into a sea she was not yet equipped to survive.

I needn't have worried. Cecily's response when I gently placed her in the water of Pretty Marsh Harbor near our home was a series of distressed barks and snorts and a valiant attempt at climbing up my legs to escape the horrible wet stuff. My thoughts went instantly from worrying about a premature dash for freedom to what I would do with a seal who hated the sea.

Twice a day I drove Cecily to the harbor and led her into the ocean, hoping she would eventually acquire a taste for the aquatic life, but she made little progress. At her most daring she would uncurl her flippers from around my achingly cold legs and swim around me in tight circles like a fat little shark. But as soon as I tried to sneak out of the water, she was at my heels.

It was clear that Cecily was not going to be doing any serious swimming without me at her side, and it was equally clear that with the water temperature at about fifty-two degrees I wasn't going to be giving any oceanic swimming lessons. I did think I might tolerate the slightly warmer lake water and wondered if fresh water was harmful to seals. Steve Katona assured me she would be fine as long as I dunked her in the ocean afterward.

The following morning I drove Cecily to a secluded area on a large lake near our home. At first she retreated as she had in the harbor—clinging to me or, at most, making quick shallow dives to investigate my toes. But she stayed by me as I waded deeper and, finally, plunged headfirst into the icy water. When I came up for air I found myself nose-to-nose with a very happy little seal. The expression on her puppylike face—her bead-black eyes and silly grin—said as clearly as words that she was thrilled to have finally coaxed me into the water!

I watched in admiring wonder as Cecily suddenly came into her own. Her two sets of flippers, which worked so clumsily on dry land, were transformed into wings. She flew through the water, performing belly rolls, nosedives and somersaults. She skimmed along the bottom like a submarine, then soared to the surface with an explosion of fine sparkling spray. After every stunt she'd swim back to me and nudge my cheek or shoulder with her whiskered nose as if to seek my approval.

Tired from treading water for more than a half-hour, I

rolled over and floated on my back for a while. Cecily, too, must have been exhausted after all those athletic shenanigans and seized the opportunity to climb onto my belly, where she lay her head on my chest and fell asleep. In the wild, Cecily and her real mother would have let the ocean rock them like this for hours. As it was, I could only stand the cold lake for a few more minutes. This time when I walked out of the water, Cecily lingered for a while in the shallows, performing a couple more graceful belly rolls before lumbering back onto dry land.

For the next few weeks, the playful little seal and I led double lives. During the day I joined her in her watery world, either swimming with her in the lake or watching her frolic about in the harbor. She no longer needed my company when she swam and would play alone in the waves, occasionally encouraging me with raucous whoops to come join her.

In the evening Cecily became part of my dry world. She often draped herself over my lap in the living room, nursing from her bottle and watching late-night TV with me.

It was an idyllic time. Somehow we had managed to find a happy compromise between her needs as an aquatic mammal and mine as a land mammal. I'm not sure what lasting lessons Cecily learned from *The Tonight Show,* but the wonders she showed me will stay with me forever.

While Cecily and I had been enjoying ourselves, a researcher had been observing a wild harbor seal colony off the shores of Mount Desert Island. She was monitoring the activities of the mothers and their pups and passing the information to me so I could base my behavior with Cecily on this model. When the researcher reported the mother seals were leaving their pups for longer and longer intervals, it was time for me to follow their example and start the painful separation of our two worlds.

Now I began taking Cecily down to the harbor in the

mornings and leaving her there for four or five hours, at which time I would return with her afternoon bottle. Every lobsterman rowing into the dock those afternoons would see a wild-haired woman waving a pink plastic baby bottle at the sea and crying out, "Sessileeeee!"

It soon became apparent that Cecily had learned to catch and eat her own fish, since it took her longer and longer to respond to my calls, and she often didn't seem that interested in the bottle—just the cuddle that came with it. When she was down to just two bottles a day, I started leaving her out all night. I missed our cozy sessions in front of the TV, but I had to accept that our two worlds were drifting apart.

"The mothers are weaning their pups," the researcher reported. It was news I was both expecting and half hoping I would never hear. It meant it was time to wean Cecily from the bottle—and from me.

On a beautiful June morning, I picked Cecily up at the harbor for the last time. Instead of giving her the expected bottle, I drove her to a private cove facing the wild colony and—as the researcher had instructed—painted a yellow stripe on her back so she could identify Cecily from the dozens of other seal pups in the area. When I waded into the water, Cecily trailed after me, reminding me with plaintive little whoops that I had forgotten her bottle. While playing with her for the last time in the shallow water of the cove, I felt what any foster parent must feel as they return a child they have grown to love to the natural parent. I caught myself feeling angry with the harsh choice that had been forced upon me. Why couldn't I just go on loving and caring for Cecily for the next twenty or thirty years?

Ultimately, though, it was Cecily who made the choice for me. Bored with my melancholic, halfhearted play, she decided to explore this new place I had brought her to and started swimming toward the open water. I desperately wanted to call her back, but I didn't. Instead I watched as her little, black head glided out of the cove toward the wild colony and, I hoped, a new life.

*Nan Lincoln*

# Surrogate Mom and Pup

Several years ago, on a cold and foggy morning in Monterey, a baby sea otter washed up on the shore of the Pacific Grove coastline, its mother nowhere in sight. The little otter had been discovered by a beachgoer who called in the field response team from the sea otter research and conservation program at the Monterey Bay Aquarium. After a thorough examination by a resident veterinarian, it was determined that the three-week-old pup was in shock and suffering from hypothermia. Even if it recovered, the veterinarian said that without a "mom" to teach it, its chances for survival in the wild were slim.

The otter, who became known as Elwood, was warmed and given antibiotics. When he finally regained consciousness, he let out a bloodcurdling cry that continued for hours on end. He wasn't interested in the aquarium-made formula, and while he managed to choke down a few morsels of clam, rock cod and squid, all he seemed to really want was his mom. As his healing progressed, Elwood was moved to an outdoor tank where he could swim. But even there the desperate pup spent most of his time searching the tank for his mother, crying in hope of some response.

Jake, the other orphaned otter who shared Elwood's tank, began to show signs of agitation from the cries, so Elwood was moved to a temporary nursery in the dive locker room on the third floor of the aquarium. Sleeping only thirty to forty minutes at a time, he continued to lament the loss of his mother. He refused contact with any human and was only quiet when he slept or ate.

Then fate intervened. While tagging sea otters to track and research for the aquarium's field research project, a group of biologists tried to catch a battered female carrying a small pup. The feisty mother wriggled free at the last moment, but left the pup. Upon closer examination, the biologists discovered the pup had been dead for a day or so, the cause of death unknown. Not giving up, the mother swam around the boat, crying for the baby. The biologists tried to draw her nearer by placing the pup in the water, but the frightened otter only swam backward toward a bed of kelp, all the while calling for her baby. The team tried again. Again the otter evaded them until all the team could do was note the distinguishing nose scar and mottled color of the otter to identify her later.

That afternoon, a member of the team, researcher Michelle Staedler, returned to the aquarium nursery to find sea otter program supervisor Julie Hymer preparing for an evening shift with Elwood. Michelle had an idea. "Hey, Julie," she said. "Do you want a mom for your pup?"

Julie looked skeptical.

"You've got one?" Julie said. "Just like that?"

"Maybe," Michelle said. "We found an otter in the bay with a dead pup. We got the pup, but the mother got away. She's swimming around the kelp screaming for her baby. And you've got a pup screaming for his mom. Why don't we try to bring them together?"

It was almost evening. The team would have to work fast. Elwood was shuffled into a kennel, screaming at the top of his lungs, and moved onto the inflatable boat the team used. The team arrived at Lover's Point, where the otter mom was last spotted. As the boat approached the point, Elwood's cries caught the attention of the mother.

Elwood was placed in the water. He began to swim toward the otter. This was the moment of truth. The otter immediately placed Elwood on her belly and began to groom him as she moved through the kelp beds. Elwood even tried to nurse. Then the female dove. Because Elwood was still buoyant in his pup coat, he was unable to follow her under the water. All he could do was swim at the surface in the direction he thought the mother was heading. Julie, Michelle and the team wondered what to do. Did the mother abandon him when she realized he wasn't hers? Could she even tell that it was the wrong pup? The adoption didn't seem to be working. The team waited. If the female had lost interest, little Elwood would not survive the night alone in the bay. Disappointed, the team moved in to rescue him.

Suddenly, the mother reappeared at the surface, snatched Elwood under her paw and swam quickly away. In seconds, the pair was safely nestled amid the kelp beds in Lover's Point. The team had done all it could do. Now it was up to Elwood's adopted mother. Cautiously, the team moved away.

The next morning both Elwood and his new mom were spotted in the area off Lover's Point. Elwood rode happily on her belly as she skulled backwards through the kelp beds. The team couldn't believe it. Sea otter mom without pup, pup without mom—the match had been made. A new family had taken residence in Monterey Bay!

*Roxayne Spruance and Michelle Staedler*

# Hooked on Mahogany

*We share the Earth not only with our fellow human beings, but with all the other creatures.*

Dalai Lama

Now that I'm old, I come to the dock with my poles and tackle, and I fish each day. There are always four or five pelicans that sit nearby on the pier and wait with great patience until I toss a fish their way. They have curious eyes with yellow irises and black pupils. Their bodies are a silvery brown, and their huge shovel mouths all seem identical. Almost all of the pelicans have large, arched necks that are white, but one is different. He seems older, wiser, something like myself. He is the lone one with a deep brown neck. I've even named him; I call him Mahogany.

There are days when the tide is out and the water is very low, but I still come around to watch him swoop in and gently land on the planks. Some mornings I fish with squid for bait and quickly hook a fish that brings Mahogany to his feet. I hold it in my hand and try to coax him, get him close. But he's a wild creature, and no amount of bribing can make him a friend. I guess I'm useful so long as I toss him a fish. Every morning we have a new encounter. One day my light pole was bending in half with the weight of a big fish. I saw Mahogany glide across the calm sea, drop daintily to the dock and watch the struggle that was going on.

The fish was tiring me, but it finally broke water, and I could see it was a hefty jack cravalle. As soon as it hit the deck, the fish and I were surrounded by a wave of young white-necked pelicans. They were in a frenzy for the jack, but calm old Mahogany just sat there and watched. I had to drive the birds away with a wave of my arms and then bucket the struggling fish. Mahogany never budged, and when the rest flew off, I cut the fish into chunks that I knew he could catch. I tossed piece after piece into his cavernous mouth, and when he finished the last, he slunk down and rested his bill on still-wet feathers. Two old men, he and I, still hanging on.

At the end of the day, I looked up and saw a flock of egrets that looked like a thousand white butterflies. Across the cove I could see the pelicans returning from yet another expedition. Like old bombers with outstretched wings, they circled a cluster of casuarina pines that grew out of the water. One by one the great birds lowered their flap feathers in midair, stalled and, with webbed landing gear down, shuddered to a halt on flimsy branches. At the top of the tallest tree I could see Mahogany preening his wings and fixing his gaze on me. I doffed my hat in tribute.

When I came to the dock in the morning, the old bird was already sitting there. I moved my gear and put some cut mullet on the hooks. In a minute I hit something, and I had to hold on for dear life. It felt as though my arms were being torn from the sockets. Mahogany flew over to the new spot, his erect feathers signaling excitement. I finally landed the monster of a catfish and was very cautious with the dorsal and pectoral fins. Each was barbed with a hidden stiletto capable of tearing the skin to the bone. I dispatched the brute and nudged it toward the pelican. But he, too, was wary of those barbs. He snubbed his beak at the fish and walked away. I love to eat catfish and know exactly how to dress them for a tasty meal. I was also curious if Mahogany would take them defanged. With a sharp fillet knife I removed the spikes and cleaned the fish while the bird watched my every move. I tossed him a few chunks, but the usually ravenous pelican turned and again walked away.

At midday, the two of us dozed in the warmth of the winter sun. It was late in the afternoon when I awoke and was aware of a bevy of pelicans waiting for a meal. My pole bent, and they knew immediately. A few remained on the dock, but the others were already in the water, ready to pluck the fish from my line. I was afraid to pull it up. If they took it, they would get the hook also. I kept the fish underwater and waited for the exact moment. When it came, I pulled hard and watched them slash each other with their swordlike bills. As I reeled in the fish, it dropped from the line. To my horror I saw the loose hook rip into the bystander—Mahogany!

My feelings were so acute that I could almost feel the hook in my own flesh. My friend had the hook embedded in his back, and for a moment I could feel his weight hanging from the pole. I cut the line immediately, and the bird flew away with fifteen feet of line dangling from his body. My mind was racing. Could he survive with the deeply embedded hook? Would it rust? Would it infect him?

In the morning I left my poles at home and walked back to the dock, looking for Mahogany, but he was gone. No one had seen him. The poles remained in my house, and I no longer fished. I spent my days just searching for the bird with the dark brown neck.

And then one day I looked up into a steel gray sky and watched a small group of pelicans come in over the water, stretch their mighty wings, and dive into the tiny cove that was alive with small fish. Again and again they went into their steep dives and scooped up the wriggling fish, which dripped from their huge mouths. Mahogany was leading the pack, still trailing fifteen feet of nylon line. Now for the first time I got my pole, and once again I fished and watched. I had my line near a forest of mangrove whose twisted roots sheltered a variety of fish. I soon had a flaming red snapper tugging on the light pole. Sure enough, the old bird showed me his confidence by dropping down not too far away. I could see the end of the gold hook in the very center of his back. I held the fish high and coaxed Mahogany to come nearer. The huge head was not too far away when I tossed him the fish. Mahogany lunged, and I did also. I clasped him to my chest and held his bill as I ran for help. At a friend's boat we held him tightly and pulled the hook out with a pair of thin pliers. He flew up as soon as I let him loose. Those huge wings pumped a few times, and then he went into his glide. The old bird banked in a wide turn and landed back on the planks. The sun was up now and everything glowed; in minutes the still water had turned to gold. I looked into Mahogany's old yellow eyes and smiled; it was nice to have him back.

*Mike Lipstock*

# Picasso of the Sea

Many years ago I was visiting my friends at the Dolphin Research Center in the Florida Keys. The director, Mandy Rodriguez, asked if I would like to paint with some of the dolphins. I, of course, wondered how this was going to work and made my way back to a lagoon where, to my surprise, a small group of bottlenose dolphins greeted me with excitement.

As I sat on the edge of the dock and readied a set of water-based acrylic paints, the dolphins became more excited. I, too, was intrigued about collaborating with these highly intelligent mammals. If any animal on Earth besides humans could create a work of art, it would most certainly be dolphins.

I passed a paintbrush to a dolphin named Kibby, who took the handle in her mouth. Next, I held up a canvas, and she immediately began to paint with a Picasso flair, laying down each stroke with a twist of her head and, finally, a 360-degree spin. When she was done, she passed the brush back to me and watched as I painted my part.

Two very diverse marine artists, Kibby, the dolphin, and I, the human, shared a single canvas. But we discovered that we also shared something else—the spirit of joy.

Together, we had created something uniquely beautiful, a one-of-a-kind collaboration between artists of two different worlds. I told my friends on the dock later that it was just the salt that made my eyes water. But they knew how I felt about making such a wonderful connection with one of these beautiful creatures.

When the painting was finished, Kibby smiled a big dolphin grin. She nodded her head in approval of the completed work, then lifted her flukes above the surface and dived. A few seconds later she brought me the highest honor a dolphin can give, a gift from the sea—a rock!

*Wyland*

# The Blind Diver

It was one of those black nights at sea. No shade of gray separated the water from the sky, nor was there a peek of light from a distant shore. Our boat anchored in the dark as oversized swells crashed upon its hull. A huge 16 mm underwater motion-picture camera was lowered over the side to a photographer in the water. The photographer signaled that the camera was secure, and the rest of us plunged into the water, each person carrying a large underwater light tethered to the generator of our boat.

Slowly, we worked our way down through the ensnaring kelp forest, guided by the lights, until the whir of the generator stopped, the lights winked out, and we were left suspended in utter, complete blackness.

I tugged on my cable only to discover it had disconnected from the generator. Without it, there was absolutely nothing to guide me to the surface or to the boat. Suddenly, it became impossible to know which way was up or down. There was no right, no left. I was completely disoriented. A chill crept over me. My breath choked midway to my lungs. I had become engulfed in a paralyzing fear. But my survival instincts weren't ready to give up yet. *I am not going to die here,* I reassured myself. *Not now. Not this way!*

My calm prevailed and effectively saved my life. I've gone diving many times after that terrifying experience, but never at night. I could not force myself to, despite the survival lessons I had learned. However, it was on another dive that I learned what it is truly like to dive without sight. This remarkable experience occurred off the coast of Florida, where I went diving with a blind man. I had met him onboard a commercial dive boat many years ago, and although I knew him for only a few hours, he changed my life forever.

Blind from birth, he had never seen a ray of light in his entire life. For his sixty-fifth birthday, he gave himself the gift of scuba diving lessons. He said he had always dreamed of someday diving off the Florida Keys, and from the moment he first learned of scuba diving, he had been consumed with the idea of floating, weightless and free, in the inner space of the ocean.

But this was more than his first attempt at diving. It was the first time he'd ever been more than fifty miles from his home in Michigan. He had never traveled alone and had never been near the water, except in a swimming pool and, later, in a Michigan quarry where he took his qualifying dive.

Once he earned his scuba diving certification, he started calling dive shops in Florida. Each call was met with disbelief. "No way!" "Blind?" "You're kidding!" were the responses he heard over and over again.

Finally, a dive-boat captain agreed to take him diving near Key Largo. I was there as he lugged his gear onboard. The sight of this man walking down the dock with a white cane in one hand and a diving bag in the other was a surreal experience in itself.

At sea, he dressed for the dive on the teetering boat, just like the rest of us. And when one of the divers tried to help him put on his tank, he said politely, "No, I can do this. But I appreciate your thought." Then he made his way to the rail of the boat, boosted himself up and flipped backward into the water.

I imagined he must have experienced the same disorientation underwater that had filled me with terror during my earlier night dive. He was, after all, completely blind!

How did he know which way was down and which way was up?

How did he know where the fish were?

He extended his hands and opened his fingers, and soon small schools of fish swam in and out of them. It was as if they were petting him. Then a five-foot-long grouper cruised right up to him as if to say, "Let's play." The blind diver seemed to welcome the fish, caressing it as if he were petting a favorite dog.

With gloved hands he explored every rock he encountered. Inch by inch. Crevice by crevice. Nothing escaped his attention. He ascended, on time, before his air ran out, found the ladder to the boat and climbed onboard, doing everything by himself, just like the rest of us.

The deck was abuzz as the blind man described everything he "saw."

"Did you see that butterfly fish?" he said, a grin spreading across his face. "And what about that angel fish? Wasn't it delicate, and oh-so-graceful? . . . And those beautiful gigantic coral heads and their tiny little polyps! And that grouper, wasn't she something!"

I stood in amazement. He had seen more than I had!

Finally, one of the other divers blurted out, "You're not blind. You've just been fooling us."

"No," our friend said. "I'm not blind, even though my eyes don't see." Then he laughed in a way that has never left me to this day. "Sight, don't you know, comes from the heart."

*Joycebelle Edelbrock*

# In Harmony

*I have no other wish than a close fusion with nature, and I desire no other fate than to have worked and lived in harmony with her laws.*

Claude Monet

When we were growing up, my dad told us many stories about the islands he had learned throughout his life. The Hawaiians are people who love the land, sky and sea, and their existence depends on its harmony. The locals who grew up in the islands have a deep respect for their beliefs. We hear all kinds of tales and legends, and we choose to believe in them.

For years and years, the locals thought the reefs and deep ocean surrounding the islands would always hold an abundance of fish. The reefs were full of manini, papio, kumu, mullet and weke, and the deeper water held the ulua and ahi.

But times changed, and more people were living in the islands. Slowly, the people noticed that each time they went fishing, they came back with fewer fish. Some of these people depended on the sea to put food on their tables and money in their pockets.

Everyone seemed to have problems catching enough fish—everyone except one man. All would watch him go out alone early in the morning and, as the sun began to set, he'd come home with more fish than anyone. *How did he do it?* They all asked each other questions, but no one wanted to ask him. No one seemed brave enough to follow and see where he went. It became more and more of a mystery, and the word began to spread. There was one fisherman who could bring in plenty of fish, while all others struggled to make a living.

Eventually, the story reached the mainland where a sport-fishing writer heard about this Hawaiian fisherman. He was determined to find out how this man was able to accomplish what no one else could, so he flew to the islands and made a surprising discovery.

On the island of Maui, he met a man with a gentle spirit who had a great respect for the sea. The sea gave him all that he needed, and he gave back part of what he had. This intrigued the writer enough to ask the questions no one else dared to ask.

The fisherman sat him down on the cool evening sand and began his story. When he was done, the writer couldn't believe what he had heard. The fisherman then quietly invited him to go out in the morning to see with his own eyes what his heart couldn't believe.

Early the next morning before the sun rose, the writer met the fisherman and climbed aboard the boat with his camera, determined to record the truth. They set off into the silent darkness with just a glimmer of light on the horizon.

They had followed the coastline for two or three miles when the fisherman cut his engine. The fisherman explained to the writer that no matter what happened, he was not to talk, just watch. Going to the side of the boat, the fisherman slapped the side a few times. He waited for a few moments and did it again. Then shielding his eyes from the early morning rays, he pointed into the far-off distance. The only thing the writer could see on the glassy water was a ripple coming toward them.

The rippling stopped, and the writer looked at the fisherman, who motioned him to wait. In a few moments, the fisherman leaned over the side and placed his hand in the water. Then from the depth of the sea, the writer could see something silvery coming toward the surface. He was shocked to see a five-foot barracuda. Unbelievable! And the fisherman had his hand in the water, just waiting. Speechless, the writer watched as the barracuda came up to the fisherman's hand and allowed him to rub its head.

When the barracuda swam away, the fisherman started up his engine and followed it. After a while, the barracuda began to swim in a big circle. The fisherman dropped his net inside the circle. Time passed, and finally the net was ready to be hoisted in. The fisherman looked through the catch, grabbed the biggest fish and dropped it into the water as the barracuda appeared to say thanks with a flip of its tail. The writer stared in amazement. *Incredible,* was all he could think.

The fisherman explained that the ritual had begun long ago, when he was out one day and a barracuda had come up to the side of his boat. This went on for years, until the time came when he noticed the barracuda was getting older and slower in his movements. He knew that some time soon, he wouldn't be seeing his friend from the sea.

One day he went out, slapped the side of his boat and saw not one rippling, but two. Alongside his old friend was a younger barracuda. The old one let the fisherman rub his head, then nudged the younger one closer to the boat, as the fisherman cautiously put his hand into the water to rub his new friend's head. Then the old one slowly swam away.

The next time the fisherman went out, along came his new friend, alone. He leaned over to rub its head as his tears fell into the sea. He knew he would never see his dear old friend again.

Never in his whole life had the writer heard such a story, but now he believed. Now his heart believed. And now he had a greater respect for the sea—and the special part of life that keeps us in harmony with nature.

*Martha Gusukuma-Donnenfield*

# Encounter with a Sperm Whale

Back in 1981, few people—if any—had swum with sperm whales: forty- to eighty-foot-long masters of the deep sea with enormous jaws containing rows of large, conical teeth. Sperm whales are elusive. They dive hundreds to possibly thousands of feet and seldom initiate contact with humans, unlike the gray or humpback whales.

We were off the coast of Sri Lanka in a small thirty-three-foot sailing vessel following pods of sperm whales for extended periods of time under the auspices of the World Wildlife Fund. The longest we managed to do this was for a few days, and it was difficult, relentless work because we had to rely on tracking their sounds. Because the whales dive for over an hour sometimes, we could not rely on sight. So we rigged up an underwater acoustic system that could locate the whales' sounds by receiving the clicks emitted from the foreheads and jaws of the whales to obtain a fix on their position. Of course, the whales sometimes "shut up," at which point it was highly possible that we would lose the group. But often we were successful, and when we followed the sounds correctly, the whales would surface in the vicinity of our little ship.

In the process of following individual whales, it was important to know if we were following males or females, so the obvious move was to go and have a look. I, of course, was dying to swim with these enormous beings, so I immediately offered to jump in. With wry humor and twinkles in their eyes, Doctors Hal Whitehead and Jonathan Gordan, my two British companions, reminded me that sperm whales "stun" their prey. The whales feed on the mysterious deep-sea giant squid, a creature that can reach sixty feet in length. The whales stun the squid, then use their long, narrow mouths to delicately seize their mouthful of food. All of this happens in darkness, possibly a thousand or more feet underwater.

And here we were, in the tropics of the Indian Ocean, dabbling with the delights of swimming with the "gentle" beings of the deep. How did we know they were gentle? Why, I might be just the size of a delectable baby squid paddling about on the surface of the water with the bright tropical sun making me an obvious target! *Of course, the sperm whale will know better than that,* I convinced myself. Furthermore, I was tantalized by the possibility of swimming with one of the largest and most elusive creatures on Earth!

I hastened on my snorkel gear, hand-hoisted myself over the stern of the thirty-three-foot sloop, tying myself to a hemp rope fastened to the stern of the ship that would pull me through the water. I had been trained a few hurried moments before about the little Nikonos camera that I held in my right hand while holding on to the rope with my left hand. I was supposed to take a picture of the genitals of the whale to identify it as a male or female. *No problem,* I thought.

I could see the outline of the ship's hull as she plowed through the blue Sri Lankan tropical water with nothing else around her, not a fish or drifting seaweed. I relaxed and enjoyed the rush through the water when I noticed the flukes of a sperm whale slowly appearing about ten feet ahead of the ship's port bow. The whale was hardly moving, swimming without seeming to notice the noisy propelled ship approaching it. Its massive body was awesome, majestic and powerful, yet it inspired no fear in me. The engines of the ship stopped as I glided alongside the gray body. I held on to my rope in silence.

The whale and I passed no more than four feet from each other. Its enormous head was larger than my entire body, and its right eye was about the size of my fist. As it cruised by we looked directly at one another. It stared openly at me, envelopng me in its gaze. In those still moments we met, two beings, me and the sperm whale. I felt accepted, and it was from this meeting that the magical world of these gray, wrinkled creatures captivated me and drew me year after year into the vastness of their watery world.

*Gaie Alling*

"Don't you think it's time we told him he's adopted?"

# Swimming Surprise

I entered the cool waters of East Rockaway inlet for my long daily swim—an hour's struggle against the current. This was usually a time for quiet reflection, with my consciousness lulled by the rhythm of arms lifting, stretching, and pulling of legs beating and driving, and of my head rhythmically turning left, center, right. Thoughts of tomorrow, today and yesterday seemed to slip quietly away in a steady stream. I could not say what prompted me to tilt my head below.

Nothing from all my years in the sea had prepared me for what I saw. As a scuba diver I had squeezed into a cave of sleeping sharks, hitched a ride on the back of a sea turtle and faced the hooded stare of a green moray eel. Long-distance surface swimming had provided its own surprises: a school of arm-sized barracuda spearing through the sea in Cozumel, a seven-foot-wide manta ray flapping its wings along the coast of a New Jersey resort, and most recently a gang of sharks scavenging along a Rockaway jetty. But this was an inlet, and I was just thirty yards from the beach. Nothing as large as what I had seen could possibly be here! I righted my head, counted five strokes, then one-two-three-four-five more, and looked down again.

We care about your opinions. Please take a moment to fill out this Reader Survey card and mail it back to us. As a special **"thank you"** we'll send you exciting news about interesting books and a valuable **Gift.**

## Please PRINT using ALL CAPS

Name
First ⎕⎕⎕⎕⎕⎕⎕⎕⎕⎕⎕⎕⎕⎕⎕⎕⎕ MI. ⎕ Last Name ⎕⎕⎕⎕⎕⎕⎕⎕⎕⎕⎕⎕⎕⎕⎕⎕⎕

Address ⎕⎕⎕⎕⎕⎕⎕⎕⎕⎕⎕⎕⎕⎕⎕⎕⎕⎕⎕⎕⎕⎕⎕⎕⎕⎕⎕⎕⎕⎕⎕⎕

City ⎕⎕⎕⎕⎕⎕⎕⎕⎕⎕⎕⎕⎕⎕⎕⎕⎕⎕⎕ ST ⎕⎕ Zip ⎕⎕⎕⎕⎕ — ⎕⎕⎕⎕

Phone # ( ⎕⎕⎕ ) ⎕⎕⎕ — ⎕⎕⎕⎕ Fax # ( ⎕⎕⎕ ) ⎕⎕⎕ — ⎕⎕⎕⎕

Email ⎕⎕⎕⎕⎕⎕⎕⎕⎕⎕⎕⎕⎕⎕⎕⎕⎕⎕⎕⎕⎕⎕⎕⎕⎕⎕⎕⎕⎕⎕⎕⎕

**(1) Gender:**
⎕ Female    ⎕ Male

**(2) Age:**
⎕ 12 or under    ⎕ 40-59
⎕ 13-19          ⎕ 60+
⎕ 20-39

**(3) Marital Status**
⎕ Married
⎕ Single
⎕ Divorced/Widowed

**(4) Did you receive this book as a gift?**
⎕ Yes    ⎕ No

**(5) How many Chicken Soup books have you bought or read?**
⎕ 1    ⎕ 2-4    ⎕ 5+

**(6) How did you find out about this book?**
*Please fill in ONE.*
1) ⎕ Recommendation
2) ⎕ Store Display
3) ⎕ Bestseller List
4) ⎕ Online
5) ⎕ Advertisement
6) ⎕ Catalog/Mailing
7) ⎕ Interview/Review (TV, Radio, Print)

**(7) Where do you usually buy books?**
*Please fill in your top TWO choices.*
1) ⎕ Bookstore
2) ⎕ Religious Bookstore
3) ⎕ Online
4) ⎕ Book Club/Mail Order
5) ⎕ Price Club (Costco, Sam's Club, etc.)
6) ⎕ Retail Store (Target, Wal-Mart, etc.)

**(9) What subjects do you enjoy reading about most?** Rank only *FIVE. Use 1 for your favorite, 2 for second favorite, etc.*

| | 1 | 2 | 3 | 4 | 5 |
|---|---|---|---|---|---|
| 1) Parenting/Family | ○ | ○ | ○ | ○ | ○ |
| 2) Relationships | ○ | ○ | ○ | ○ | ○ |
| 3) Recovery/Addictions | ○ | ○ | ○ | ○ | ○ |
| 4) Health/Nutrition | ○ | ○ | ○ | ○ | ○ |
| 5) Christianity | ○ | ○ | ○ | ○ | ○ |
| 6) Spirituality/Inspiration | ○ | ○ | ○ | ○ | ○ |
| 7) Business Self-Help | ○ | ○ | ○ | ○ | ○ |
| 8) Teen Issues | ○ | ○ | ○ | ○ | ○ |
| 9) Sports | ○ | ○ | ○ | ○ | ○ |

**(14) What attracts you most to a book?**
*(Please rank 1-4 in order of preference.)*

| | 1 | 2 | 3 | 4 |
|---|---|---|---|---|
| 14) Title | ○ | ○ | ○ | ○ |
| 15) Cover Design | ○ | ○ | ○ | ○ |
| 16) Author | ○ | ○ | ○ | ○ |
| 17) Content | ○ | ○ | ○ | ○ |

TAPE IN MIDDLE; DO NOT STAPLE

# BUSINESS REPLY MAIL
FIRST-CLASS MAIL  PERMIT NO 45  DEERFIELD BEACH, FL

POSTAGE WILL BE PAID BY ADDRESSEE

CHICKEN SOUP FOR THE OCEAN LOVER'S SOUL
HEALTH COMMUNICATIONS, INC.
3201 SW 15TH STREET
DEERFIELD BEACH FL 33442-9875

|ₗₗₗₗₗₗₗ|ₗₗₗ.ₗ.ₗ.ₗ|ₗ.ₗ.ₗ|ₗₗₗ|ₗₗₗₗₗₗₗ|ₗₗₗₗₗₗₗ|ₗₗₗ|

FOLD HERE

Comments:

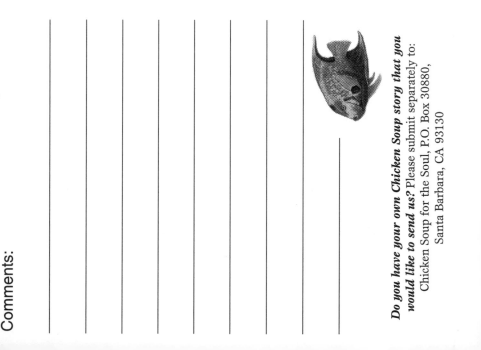

*Do you have your own Chicken Soup story that you would like to send us?* Please submit separately to:
Chicken Soup for the Soul, P.O. Box 30880,
Santa Barbara, CA 93130

It was still there—white, with a corona of milky luminescence. I longed for the familiar blurry darkness before me. White shimmering fear engulfed me. *Shark! Great white shark!* I searched for the mouth. *I had to identify the jaws.* But I couldn't see. My entire view did not extend beyond its immense underside. I strained to see its mouth, its jaws. Needing air, I raised my head and gulped, but the air was contaminated by my sudden fear of being ripped apart while in this helpless vertical position. I submerged and searched vainly for the jaws. The whiteness began to give way, replaced not by a fixed shape, but by a sense of supple, wrinkled flesh. Trying to keep it in view at all times, I cautiously moved in the direction of the shore. The whiteness dissolved. I turned around repeatedly, rotating only my hands in the puniest of breaststrokes, but still I could not see it.

Then, on the shore side within a few feet of me, it appeared. Instinctively, I drew my legs up and into my body, watching and waiting, only a deep pulsing in my throat breaking the stillness. Slowly, ponderously, it rolled past me. This was no shark. It could only be a whale—a *white* whale! It dipped sharply, reversed direction and rose in a long, twisting figure eight. Again and again it made passes at me, always too close for me to gauge its size. I surfaced, stared down and saw nothing. The whale circled, circumscribing orbits about me with celestial precision. *He's playing with me. He doesn't want to hurt me,* I said to myself reassuringly. I took a stroke toward the beach, but my intention was rudely dismissed. How had he passed within inches of my face without touching my outstretched arms? With an inverted underwater butterfly scoop, I retreated. He passed, and I withdrew farther. Why hadn't I sighted the distance to the beach? There, I knew, sunbathers were rubbing their bodies with lotions and oils, and the voices of splashing children reached my ears.

I shuddered from the cold. Were we in deeper waters? How far out had the current drawn me? He might not ever let me back to shore! All my life I had been more comfortable in the water than out, but now I realized that I could never be more than an adopted child of the sea and that I wanted land, home.

So closely did he glide past me that I blinked, so slowly that I followed his flawless design—his tail, which could crush me if it flexed near my head and could puncture my eardrums. I recalled a high-school teammate emerging from the pool with blood dripping from his ear, a casualty of a mere swimmer's butterfly kick. I was a swimmer, I reminded myself. Swim.

I stroked twice, full determined strokes. The water became murky, as if full of sand. I lowered my feet and felt the bottom. Splashing my way out of the waist-deep water, I shouted "Whale! Whale!" to the fishermen strung along the curved beach. "There's a whale in there!" But the curious state of relaxed concentration of the fishermen, their silent dialogue with the sea, prevailed. Then two hundred yards from the shore, a gray-white rolling hump broke the water's surface, submerged and broke through once again. The fishermen, as if their lines had been snared and dragged to that spot, turned their bodies, pointed their poles and stared. This was one "fish" that no one would catch.

*Joseph Hallstein*

# If You Could Touch a Whale

It was early March, and our small, wooden skiff was almost the color of the cloudless Mexican sky as we waded through shallow water and hiked ourselves over the side.

Once again, Laguna San Ignacio was filled with wintering gray whales—the same grays that had once been named "devilfish" by terrified whalers. But instead of hugging the shoreline that day, as superstitious local fishermen had done for more than a century, we boldly headed into their midst, carefully scanning for spouts.

Suddenly, a huge head surfaced within inches of the boat, rising to the level of our faces. A single unnerving eye stared. A mouth, more than seven feet long, curved downward in a perpetual frown as though warning us that we were invading. Eighty thousand pounds of whale were poised motionless next to a tiny panga holding a woman, a single fisherman and a slender twelve-year-old girl named Rhiannon.

For a split second no one breathed. And then Rhiannon and I simultaneously reached out and began caressing the scarred, rubbery face of the huge creature.

Between the clusters of barnacles, its skin was smooth, slick and pleasant to the touch, like a wet surfboard. And surprisingly soft. When we massaged, it gave a bit, like an inner tube.

Yes, we massaged. We stroked. We cooed and crooned. We slid our hands inside the lips of this giant creature and rubbed vigorously. We knelt in the bottom of the boat and laid our cheeks against the cheek of what was once considered a monster, and she didn't move away. And when this beautiful whale raised her head to face us, head-on, both of us leaned forward and kissed her.

Moments later, in open water, the same whale would splash and churn and turn exuberant side rolls, huge flippers foaming up white water in movements that would certainly have smashed the skiff had she been closer. Then she would return to us for another petting with a delicacy of movement that seemed impossible in an animal so huge.

The contact was exhilarating. So much so that, at one point, our fisherman guide had to grab the back of Rhiannon's life jacket and hold on to her. So intensely involved had the fearless preteen become in stroking this wonderful whale that she inadvertently began to crawl over the bow of the boat and onto the whale's head. The whale remained perfectly still until the youngster was fully back in the boat.

It was, as Rhiannon would say over and over, "the best day of my life!"

But how dare I, an admittedly intrepid adult traveler, expose a child to the dangers of contact with wild whales in open water, on a sometimes choppy sea?

Never for a moment did I consider her in danger, for I had been to Laguna San Ignacio before. And I will return again and again and again. You see, there is simply no experience in the world like touching a wild whale—a whale that seems to want to be your friend.

A lot has changed since the mid-1800s, when the grays earned their fearsome reputation by fighting their relentless and methodical slaughter by whalers in this very same lagoon. But the great beasts were never a match for man, and the clear blue waters of today then ran red with the blood of dying mothers and calves. By the 1930s, the whales had been hunted almost to extinction. The handful of remaining grays had no reason to trust man and every reason to fear him.

No one really knows why the grays of Laguna San Ignacio first began approaching humans for contact in the 1970s, but each year the number of "friendlies" has increased. Today, as many as four hundred whales gather here at a time, and awesome is still the only word that adequately describes how one feels in their midst.

Each time I have visited, whales of every size and age surround our boat whenever we take to the water, so many that it's sometimes hard to know where to look next. Whales spouting, sleeping, mating, breaching. Whales with babies. Whales spyhopping to check out the humans.

One by one, the friendlies come to the boat to be touched and stroked and applauded. Forty-ton females bring their one-ton calves and patiently, by example, teach the extremely shy newborns to come directly to our outstretched hands.

During those long, marvelous, sun-baked days each winter, I have tickled the tummies of some of the largest mammals on Earth. I have gotten so close, hanging over the side of the boat, that I've looked straight down blowholes into the dark interiors of whales.

Scientists can't explain, but the fishermen who live with these whales know. And those of us who come here often also know. It is very simple.

We have changed. And they have forgiven us.

*Paula McDonald*

# Back to Sea . . . the Story of J. J.

Having been fortunate enough to have worked with animals all around the world, I've been touched by many, many great wildlife "moments." But none has been quite as rewarding as the saga of a baby female whale named J. J.

It was January 11, 1997, when a nearly comatose infant gray whale was rescued from a beach near Los Angeles, California. Local marine-mammal specialists combined efforts with Sea World of San Diego, and the big baby was rushed to a holding tank at Sea World. The vets who examined the whale said the prognosis was poor, but at least this way it would have a chance to pull through. Helping it back into the water at the beach would have meant sure death.

The process of moving the whale went without a hitch, and soon the one-and-a-half-ton, fourteen-foot-long whale, nicknamed J. J., was under the watchful eyes of experts twenty-four hours a day. She must have liked her new home because she began responding quickly. She was hungry (the best sign from an ailing animal), and she was drinking six liters of whale milk substitute every three hours!

After three days she had gained eighty pounds and

weighed in at 1,750 pounds. Even with hopes high, however, the prospect of treating an infant whale in critical condition was daunting. The staff at Sea World was expert in treating marine mammals, but they had never worked with a gray whale. Yet J. J. was defying the odds. Two weeks after the rescue, she was moved into a massive 1.7 million-gallon pool where her health continued to improve. At one year, she tipped the scales at 17,000 pounds and was twenty-nine feet in length. With her gargantuan appetite, she was consuming over eight hundred pounds of fish a day.

Of course, the media was delighting in this "feel-good," animal-interest story, and soon visitors wanted to see J. J. in the flesh. People came from everywhere to see her. I could hardly believe she was swimming and cavorting in the water much as she would in the ocean! I had to consider what a special experience this was . . . few people are fortunate enough to watch whales in the wild. I've caught glimpses of them breaking the surface only occasionally. But the chance to observe a gray whale firsthand at close quarters was a memory I would always cherish. Even at her young age, her size and grace in the water amazed me!

J. J. was lucky to have met some human friends who cared enough to spend countless hours—and dollars—to save her, but her future would be to live with other gray whales in the wild blue waters. The Sea World biologists and trainers weaned her from the milk formula to a diet of squid and fish, the same food she would encounter in the wild. They even taught her how to scoop fish into her mouth and use her baleen to filter out water and sediment.

In late March 1998, the Sea World staff readied their new friend for release into the ocean, but many questions were still unanswered. Would all the training and conditioning be adequate for her new life at sea? Would she try to meet wild whales, and if so, would she be integrated into a pod?

We could only hope for the best. J. J. had been taught to live in the wild, and now was her time. Early on March 31, she was loaded onto a specially outfitted eighteen-wheel truck and driven along Interstate 5 to the release site. Need I say that this was, indeed, an unusual sight, especially with a police escort! Finally, the truck toting the eight-ton whale approached the pier, and J. J. was loaded onto a ship that headed for deep water. The day was overcast, but as we arrived at the release point, the sun seemed to magically appear.

The enormous nylon sling that held J. J. was lifted from the ship, then lowered into the awaiting ocean—and with a swish of her huge tail, J. J. was gone! She had defied the odds. This was the first time in history that a near-dead baby whale had been nursed to health and released back to sea. I kept thinking that so much could have happened to her along the way, from her not being rescued from the beach in time, to rejecting the milk formula and other care she received, to not accepting training and conditioning.

I'm sure that today she is doing just fine in the waters of the Pacific. Go whale-watching sometime and say hello if you see her!

*Jack Hanna*

*Northern Waters*

*Original painting by Wyland* ©2003.

# Keiko the Whale

*We ourselves feel that what we are doing is just a drop in the ocean. But the ocean would be less because of that missing drop.*

Mother Teresa

If you have kids, you've probably seen the movie *Free Willy* about a boy who saves a young orca from the clutches of an unscrupulous owner. But in real life Free Willy was far from free. The orca, whose real name was Keiko, was captured in the Atlantic Ocean, near Iceland, and lived in captivity after the filming of the movie in a small cement pool at an amusement park in Mexico City. The conditions of the park were poorly suited to an animal of this size, and Keiko developed a skin disease that resulted in lesions throughout his body.

Here was literally the biggest movie star in the world, sick and languishing. If something wasn't done quickly, Keiko's future looked grim. Fortunately, word of Keiko's situation was spreading rapidly around the world. Many people wanted to help, and so did I.

I had been introduced to Keiko through the Mexican

tourism authority at Keiko's residence at the Reino Aventura Park in Mexico City. The minute I leaned over the holding tank and saw the five-ton animal, I knew I had to do something . . . quick. His flippers and flukes were covered with skin growths, and he was thousands of pounds underweight. It sounds kind of strange, but Keiko and I bonded. As I scratched him I said that I would return and do everything I could to make sure he was returned to his native waters off Iceland.

In exchange for his release, I agreed to paint a giant public mural of Keiko swimming free with his family at the entrance to the park. A few months after the mural was completed, Keiko was moved to a larger, temporary home at the Oregon Coast Aquarium to recuperate and prepare for his return to Iceland. Eventually, he gained weight and learned how to catch live fish. He was ready to be flown back to the cool waters of his northern home. Millions of children who had raised nickels and dimes to save Keiko were now keeping their fingers crossed, hoping that Keiko would soon be reunited with his orca family in the wild.

The transition took some time. Keiko continued to undergo rehabilitation in a special baypen near Iceland's Westman Islands and eventually began to take more interest in his natural environment. For the first two years, he seemed content to travel back and forth between his pen and the wild ocean, not quite certain about what to do with the strange underwater wilderness to which he had been returned. There was certainly nothing human about it, and for most of his life, that was all he had known. Then, during a training rendezvous with a small pod of orcas at the southernmost tip of the Westmans, Keiko bolted toward open sea. This time, however, he didn't turn back. A satellite transmitter indicated later that he was headed for Norway and soon had taken up an active, healthy residence in Taknes Bay. Suddenly, for the first time since his capture more than twenty-two years ago, Keiko was not in a captive facility or a netted pen. His decisions were now guided by instinct and his innate orca intelligence— an intelligence that we have yet to fully comprehend.

No one can say for certain what the future holds for this special whale whose journey has taken him so far. But I, like millions of others, am hoping that after all these years of captivity, he can adapt and thrive in the wild and become truly free—not in the way of some Hollywood script—but as nature intended from the very beginning.

*Wyland*

"Matthew, did we agree to adopt a whale?"

# Angus

*It is an old dream:* To travel on the back of a benevolent sea beast down to some secret underwater garden.

Stephen Harrigan

In June 1999, I was filming California sea lions at a rookery on Los Islotes in the Sea of Cortez with my friend and fellow marine biologist Seth Schulberg. Every day we took the scenic road out of La Paz, Mexico, past the fuming harbor of Pichilingue to the playa beyond, where we met our skipper, an Antonio Banderas look-alike named Jose Antonio. We began a session of calisthenics that consisted of passing two tons of cameras, dive gear and gas tanks from the car to the boat. From there we bounded through the Canal de San Lorenzo in our equipment-laden panga, toward the breathtaking desert island bluffs of Espiritu Santo and Isla Partida, until the foghorn of sea lions and their bleating, shivering pups announced the presence of Los Islotes.

The Mexican government had granted us permission to film, provided that we worked sensitively and did not cause undue disturbance. I had stationed myself in the water next to a huge, angular boulder and was getting good footage of the big dominant sea lion bulls when a four-thousand-pound male elephant seal appeared out of nowhere and charged at me with the obvious intent of inhaling me.

Strangely enough, while my face rested on the tongue of this animal, I remember recalling other stories of aggressive male elephant seals and that very little underwater footage existed of them. And, of course, there was the little issue of trying to figure out the proper response to this attack. There really wasn't much else to do except let this enormous seal choke on me. I went limp. To my relief, the seal let go of my head. He was now looking at me with large, intense black eyes. Then his giant nose inflated, and he tried to swallow my head once more. This time, however, I gave him my camera instead.

Was he playing? Was this some kind of a secret elephant seal greeting ritual? Was he, gulp, aroused? And what was he doing in the Sea of Cortez? I knew that elephant seals are partial to the cold, rich waters of the Pacific Ocean. I had to wonder if this one was lost. My brain was running at high speed. Should I film this rare encounter, or should I flee to the safety of the boat? The giant seal appeared calm and friendly, and while he repeatedly tried to grab my head, he did so in a very gentle manner. So, what the heck, I stayed. When he came up from behind me, I wondered, yet again, if I had made the wrong decision. He wrapped his flippers around me in an elephant seal version of a bear hug from which there was no escape. But again, he let me go without even scratching the camera lens. Eventually, he grew bored with me, and after twenty-five minutes he took off. *Chewing on a big camera must not have been much fun after all*, I thought.

Back at the boat, I found my friend Seth basking in the Mexican sun. He had encountered the seal, too. He said it had caught him from behind in its customary embrace. Faced with the same set of decisions, Seth opted for swooning. Once he went limp, the seal let him go. Seth said that, at first, he had no idea what had gotten hold of him. He had never been hugged that tightly in his life. He said it felt like a scene from an old prison movie. "Not to mention," he added, "that I was completely terrified." We decided at that point to name the seal. For the rest of the trip, it would be known as Angus, from the Latin name *Mirounga angustirostris.*

Later that evening, we went over the footage of the big elephant seal swimming through the waters off Los Islotes. As he moved around the camera, it became clear that Angus was exhibiting curiosity, not aggression. This unusual behavior left us counting the minutes until our next encounter. The next day, Angus greeted us as soon as we hit the water, as fascinated with our heads as ever. While I could offer the camera in lieu of mine, Seth had no camera and thus had a harder time keeping his head out of the lion's mouth, as it were. All he could do was offer up an arm and shadow box with Angus.

The giant seal took turns embracing us and dragging us through the water. He managed to totally dismantle my camera, sending floats to the surface and lights to the bottom. At one point, he grabbed Seth's arm, shook him like a doll, then swam off with Seth tucked under his flipper for a tour of the rock. On the second lap, Seth managed to recover a little dignity by rolling onto Angus's back for what looked like an elephant seal rodeo ride.

We returned for four more days. But to our disappointment, Angus's attitude had changed. His enthusiasm was gone. He seemed to want nothing more than to loll around on the rocks, his eyes relaxed and drooping, barely responding to the crabs crawling over him. Apparently, he was going to enjoy the sunshine, and that was that. With the star of our show suddenly uncooperative, we packed up our equipment and left.

The next season, Jose Antonio informed us that Angus had gone shortly after we did. Elephant seals like Angus were driven to the brink of extinction at the turn of the last century. Fortunately, their numbers are growing, as are their rookeries. Perhaps Angus was a pioneer exploring the brave new world. Maybe he was testing the reception that others of his kind would find at this barren outpost. I hope he found the experience to his liking. If he did, who knows, maybe he'll return to Los Islotes with more seals to establish the first elephant seal rookery in the Sea of Cortez.

*Florian Graner*

# Sound Behavior

It wasn't very often that I got to enjoy all of the public exhibits and presentations at the aquarium where I worked. My job was behind the scenes in the volunteer department, where I helped coordinate the schedules of over five hundred volunteers, all with very different schedules and lots of questions. So when I was at work, I was always busy.

To complicate matters, I was six months pregnant. I constantly needed to get up and move around throughout the day to keep from getting stiff. So in one of those rare moments when I wasn't swamped with work, I took a walk to the public marine-mammal presentation. As I sat in the large amphitheater waiting for the show, I wondered why I didn't do this sort of thing more often. Clamoring for a look at the otters, seals, dolphins and beluga whales in the three-million-gallon tank were groups of excited children, their parents, out-of-towners, lovebirds, the simply curious and me.

The announcer welcomed everybody and explained some of the more fascinating characteristics of marine mammals. He said, for example, that the dolphins had an amazing ability to detect size, shape, distance, texture and movement by sending out a high-pitched sound and waiting for the echo to return. He called this echolocation. Dolphins have refined this sense to such a degree that they could even recognize when another animal is pregnant by detecting fluid in the pregnant animal's amniotic sac. When the announcer said this, he caught my attention immediately.

After the show ended, I headed straight to the glass of the exhibit for a close-up view of the dolphins. I wanted to see just how refined this sense of echolocation was. Looking cool and inconspicuous, I waited for the crowd to file out of the amphitheater doors. As the area quieted, I tried to gain the attention of the dolphins. I whistled. I coughed. I grunted. I groaned. I said, "Pssst!" Nothing worked. So I did what any attention-starved individual does when nobody is looking: I started to run from one end of the glass to the other, flapping my arms up and down. After ten sprints I stopped, my heart beating fast, my breathing heavy. Puffing and panting, I looked at the pod of dolphins, expecting them to be riveted by the commotion, their powers of echolocation focused on the pregnant woman on the other side of the glass.

Nothing.

Frustrated, I went back to my office, seriously doubting the so-called phenomenon of echolocation.

Later that day, a dolphin trainer came up to me.

"Abby?" the trainer said.

"Yes."

"Can I ask you a question?"

"Sure," I said. "Do you need a volunteer for something?"

"Actually . . ." She stopped. She seemed a little reluctant to continue. "I, um, was watching you by the dolphin tank this morning. I was just wondering if you're okay."

I felt my face flush. I tried to explain my little "experiment." The trainer tried to look serious. Then, unable to hold back any longer, she erupted in laughter. She didn't seem to be showing any signs of stopping, either. Other people around us began to stare. Finally, after she caught her breath, she explained to me that echolocation definitely worked. It just didn't work like that. "You need to be in the water," she said. "That's the only way the animals can sense you."

The next day I formally requested permission to assist with a cleaning dive of the marine mammal exhibit. You can probably guess what the exhibit manager's answer was.

*Abby Murray*

*Genesis*

*Original painting by Wyland ©2003.*

# 2

# THE POWER
# TO HEAL

*Look deep into nature, and then you will
understand everything better.*

*Albert Einstein*

# Anna's Miracle

Each time the dolphins and trainers meet a new student, excitement charges the air. How will the dolphins react to the individual's personality? To his or her disability? How will the child (or adult) react to meeting a dolphin eye-to-eye for the first time? And, the most important question, will this unique experience trigger something inside the student that will open his mind and allow new learning to take place?

When we met Justin, we all wondered how these questions would be answered during his first dolphin encounter. His parents had arranged a two-week visit to Dolphin Research Center (DRC) to participate in our Dolphin/Child Therapy program. Justin had cerebral palsy, a neurological disorder. Cerebral palsy is a serious condition, causing paralysis or muscle weakness as a result of trauma to the brain. Typical symptoms, which range from mild to severe, include partial or total inability to walk, little or no speech production, seizures and generally impaired coordination.

Justin had better motor skills and coordination than many children with cerebral palsy, but one primary difficulty he had was with speech. At three years old, he had not yet spoken his first word. We hoped that the interaction with Annessa (who we nicknamed Anna) would encourage Justin to speak at least some components of words.

Justin was a beautiful child, with blond hair and green-gold eyes. When he joined the therapist, his mother and Linda (the dolphin trainer) on Anna's dock, Justin's small face was devoid of expression. It was very hard to figure out what he was feeling. Anna tried to engage Justin in play while he was on the floating dock, but he would only glance at her briefly then look away. We decided to place Justin in the water with Anna to see what progress could be made in that environment.

Floating in the warm Gulf waters, Justin's mother held him in her arms as Anna slowly circled them. Justin's eyes locked onto Anna's movement immediately. Anna offered her dorsal fin and towed Justin and his mother gently through the water. Anna then approached Justin head-on, very carefully, and he reached out a pudgy hand to touch her snout. Anna inched closer. Justin then raised his arms and gently hugged Anna's big, gray face. They held this embrace for several seconds, then the eight-foot-long dolphin delicately eased herself backward, moving with incredible care, barely rippling the water's surface. Linda watched in awe. This was not a behavior trained to Anna, but a spontaneous gesture and offering from dolphin to child.

Justin wore a solemn expression throughout the exchange, but immediately began vocalizing when Anna backed away. The therapist asked Justin to try to make specific sounds, such as the "B" sound in "baby," promising Anna's return if Justin attempted the new sound. Justin quickly caught on to the game and responded to the coaxing. After each sound he looked expectantly for his new friend Anna. She was ready and waiting with a kiss for him!

As the lesson time came to an end, Justin was much more animated than when he started. After getting out of the water, he smiled and pointed around with excitement as his mother dried him with a towel. Suddenly, he wrapped his arms around her neck and quietly said into her ear his very first word.

For any parent, hearing the first word from your baby is a magical moment. For the parent of a child with disabilities, however, that moment is much, much more. It is a miracle that brings hope for a brighter future. Most children's first word is "mama" or "dada," but Justin was different. Justin's first word was . . . "Anna."

*Linda Schnecker Erb*

# Manatee Tranquility

It was the last thing anyone expects. I had rounded the corner on my motorcycle at fifty miles an hour. Unfortunately, so did the car coming from the opposite direction. I learned later that the collision had sent me flying a hundred and seventy feet. My legs, hips and internal organs—just about every piece of my body—had been crushed. Doctors said I would never walk again. Let me tell you, there are few more sobering words in life than that. Now the question was: What was I going to do? With little else to do over the course of my recovery, I began to examine my life. A friend suggested I try boating. *Right,* I thought. *As if that was going to make a difference!* But my friend insisted. And, yes, the spring-fed rivers around my home in Florida were beautiful this time of year. The channels were fringed with Sabal palms, live oaks and southern magnolia. I was skeptical, but maybe he was right. Maybe I could spend some quiet time on the river and perhaps even find the answers to some of my questions about life.

After I was discharged and feeling a little better, I bought a kayak and volunteered my time with a local organization to teach visitors about the endangered manatees that inhabited the rivers. Every day, I would paddle through the river with my dog Sky, a two-year-old red chow, perched at the front of the kayak. Pretty soon I was enjoying the sounds of nature and talking to boaters about rules regarding manatees.

The work was comforting and relaxing, but I still couldn't escape the feeling that something was missing. Then one day while I was doing a manatee count for a local research group, I saw a tiny, wrinkled nose poke out of the river. A baby manatee, less than two weeks old, was swimming with its mother close behind. Sky's ears shot up. As I paddled toward the manatee family, Sky moved to the front of the kayak, her black tongue hanging to the side. This was her first experience with a baby manatee, and I figured she probably wanted to get a close look. The water began to bubble. Sky barked. She wanted to know exactly what this thing was. It probably looked too small to be a manatee. For all she knew, it was some chubby, little alligator. When the baby manatee finally came up, it sprayed foam all over Sky, who, for the first time in her life, looked too shocked to bark. But Sky was nothing if not a trooper. She regained her composure, leaned in again and balanced carefully until she and the baby manatee were touching noses and greeting each other like visitors from different worlds. With the mother close at hand, I reached down and scratched the little manatee. I scratched and scratched. The manatee couldn't seem to get enough. She was in absolute manatee heaven.

All that winter, Sky and I took the kayak out on the river. Pretty soon Sky and the baby manatee were greeting each other like old friends. That's when I first noticed the change. My whole outlook began to shift. I had been undergoing physical therapy all this time, and slowly, but surely, I regained full use of my legs. Eventually, I could even walk without a cane.

There was something special about those days on the water. I think I was inspired by the affinity for life all these creatures had, even the baby manatee. She had a tranquility that I'd never seen before. She just moved around with the sure and certain knowledge that things were okay. Being out there with them day after day, I began to feel like that, too. Eventually, I became certain about life again and gained the understanding that, no matter how bad things got, life would take care of itself. And that feeling has never gone away.

*Paul Dragon*
*As told to Steve Creech*

*Sacred Waters*

*Original painting by Wyland ©2003.*

# The Art of Healing

*The sea fires our imagination and rekindles our spirit.*

Wyland

It was Christmas Day 1984, and I began painting my first Whaling Wall in Hawaii. The giant blank wall, three hundred feet long and twenty stories high, faced Kaiser Hospital. Patients, many sick and dying, looked out of their windows and saw a depressing beige wall, the architects' answer to saving costs. But I saw the wall as a perfect canvas to display life-size humpback whales and other colorful marine life.

As I began painting that first day, I noticed an old man with an IV attached to his arm sitting in a wheelchair, watching my every move.

Day after day this man would come out on the balcony of his hospital room and spend nearly every moment watching me paint my largest marine mural. I would wave to him each day, and he would wave back with all the energy left in his fragile body. Four months later at the dedication of the mural, I cut the ribbon with city officials and thousands of supporters and looked across the parking lot where, among the many hospital rooms, I caught a glimpse of the old man. He tipped his hand to me for what I knew would be the last time. I tried to hold back my emotion as I waved back. I found out later from his family that he had an incurable cancer and should have died months before, but had wanted to live to see the mural completed. The man died shortly after the dedication ceremony; his memory and spirit will live with me—and within that mural—forever.

*Wyland*

# A Signal Is Worth a Thousand Words

On a bright, warm Tuesday afternoon, Alan met Merina. It was love at first sight! Twenty-four-year-old Alan, deaf and mentally challenged, was an excellent swimmer participating in a therapy session at Dolphin Research Center. He was thrilled with Merina's ability to imitate his every move. He yelled with enthusiasm when Merina dorsal-towed him through the water and laughed when she splashed saltwater in his face! The therapist, Alan's watching family and I, the dolphin trainer, all caught his enthusiasm, and everyone sported ear-to-ear grins.

As Alan climbed onto the dock after his swim, I showed him some dolphin sign language (hand signals). Since Alan speaks American Sign Language fluently, he loved the fact that dolphins understood sign as well, and he gave Merina several signals. She responded perfectly to all of his requests, until she saw an unfamiliar one. Alan presented the same sign over again to Merina, as he gazed at her with bright eyes. Merina kept touching her snout to his extended right hand, where his fingers formed a signal unfamiliar to her. Then she rose up and kissed Alan on the cheek.

Alan cheered wildly!

I turned to Alan's parents and asked, "What does that sign mean?" With tears in their eyes, they replied simply, "I love you."

*Linda Schnecker Erb*

# The Fishermen

Gateway National Park at Great Kills is located in New York City. Visitors to the park number in the tens of thousands each season. They come to fish, swim and picnic or just to stroll along the beach. As a "regular" at the park for the past thirty years, I have seen just about everything there is to see in this wonderful place. From harbor seals and sea turtles to egrets and herons, it is easy to forget that you are still within the confines of "the big city."

Every day in spring, a small group of us fish at the park for striped bass. Casual fishermen shy away when confronted with the worn look of our faces and the rough tone of our conversation. True striped bass fans work hard for their success and are reluctant to part with "privileged information." We begin around 1:00 A.M. and fish until dawn. At thirty-five years old, I was the youngest of the group. The Nelson brothers were in their early forties and still lived with their mother. Jimmy was the older of the two, a dyed-in-the-wool "bass hound" with two fifty-pounders on his resume. John was by far the loudest of our group. Recently divorced and retired, he was six feet, two inches tall and built more like a linebacker than a fisherman. John had a broad smile to go with his wit and a knack for catching huge fluke, which earned him the title

"Duke of Fluke." And, finally, there was Frank. In his late sixties and in failing health, Frank was the general target for most of John's wisecracks. Frank seemed to enjoy the attention, though. I suppose the daily verbal jousts kept Frank's mind off his problems. His wife passed away during the winter, and years of hard work had taken their toll on his body. Unable to haul heavy gear across the sand, Frank was relegated to fishing near the parking area.

We were friends in the quiet, casual way of fishermen, but we really didn't get to know each other until the spring of 1999. That was when we first noticed the little seagull with one leg. White and gray with a long slender beak and dark eyes, it swam surprisingly well, although a bit slower than the other birds. The real comedy—and what really caught our attention—began when it got on dry land. Hopping around in search of a meal, it looked like a drunk staggering home. Or, as John put it, "like Frank on a good day." We felt a little sorry for it, so we fed it some of our bait. Jimmy figured it had lost its leg to a bluefish. He was probably right. A hungry bluefish would eat anything that moves, and with its powerful jaws, there was no question it could bite a bird's leg clean off.

That was how it began. Our new mascot would go off from time to time. But he always came back, sometimes a day later, sometimes two. John would always toss some fresh fish at him and comment on how well he was doing. We figured he was a pretty tough customer, surviving on one leg. He took what life dealt him and found a way to keep going. Then one day, he showed up with a broken wing—a death sentence for a seagull. He probably had hurt himself trying to land—those one-foot landings had to be tricky. It was clear that our friend needed all the help we could give him.

Every day, the seagull waited for us to come and fish, knowing that a meal pretty much always came with the deal. When Frank offered food, it would hop toward us, its injured wing dragging behind it. John called the seagull and

Frank "birds of a feather." And when we realized that the other birds were stealing the injured gull's food, we took it upon ourselves to shoo away the hungry, healthier intruders. Deep down we knew it had no chance of surviving the winter—no matter what we did. But we chose to ignore the truth. We were determined to make the best of it. We cared for the bird as though it was a member of the family.

During this time, Frank began to open up about his wife. He seemed to accept things more. It was as though this silly bird gave him something to care about again. At some point, the bird even took Frank's place as the butt of John's jokes. Even when the fishing was better in other places, we chose not to leave. Our friend would be waiting there, happy to see us, and we didn't want to disappoint him.

The days grew shorter. The fish had already begun their fall migration. We knew the bird's days were numbered. When the fish moved south, they took our little mascot's food supply with them. In a desperate attempt to circumvent Mother Nature, John and Frank made daily trips to the beach with bread and little pieces of fish.

One day the pair came with their food, but the bird didn't show. They waited for hours. "Maybe we'll see him tomorrow," John said hopefully. But Frank knew the truth. The inevitable had come to pass. But Frank wasn't as sad as he thought he would be. The little bird had brought this solitary group of fishermen together in an unexpected way. These men, as different from one another as they could be, had cared for it, each in their own way, expecting nothing in return. The fact was, the little bird had become their friend. "No," Frank said, "I don't think we will be seeing him pass this way again." He looked out across the water. "We gave him one heck of a summer, though."

*Stephen Byrne*

# A Day on the New Hampshire Shore

*We do not associate the idea of antiquity with the ocean, nor wonder how it looked a thousand years ago, as we do of the land, for it was equally wild and unfathomable always.*

Henry David Thoreau

There were six of us in the car: me, my friend Shelley, her parents Mel and Cathy, and her aunt Pam and uncle Jay. We had made the two-day drive from Michigan to see Shelley's ill grandfather, who lived in a small town south of Portsmouth, New Hampshire. I agreed to go to keep Shelley company, and because I had never left the Midwest. Once we got there, however, a pall was cast by the condition of Shelley's grandpa. It was much more serious than we had known. It seemed that everyone who saw him returned fighting back tears. So rather than sight-seeing, we spent most of our time in the parlor sitting on the couch, talking little to each other or anyone else.

At one point, we tried to take a walk. But in a town that consisted of three buildings—a post office, a general store and a hardware store—we quickly discovered there was nowhere to go. Two days passed. I had never seen the ocean before, and Shelley's mother suggested we go to the beach for some fresh air. She and her sister Pam and their spouses decided to accompany us. The girls had spent summers in the area until their parents divorced, and they went to live with their mother in Michigan. This was their first visit back to New Hampshire in a decade.

My first sight of the ocean took my breath away: It looked cold and expansive, with a gray sky that stretched for miles above the churning blue water. I took my shoes off, despite warnings about the jagged rocks, and raced to the water's edge where the tide lapped my toes. The others joined me there, and we stood gazing for what seemed like forever. I could tell that the minds of Cathy and Pam weren't far removed from the sickroom where their father lay, and it was not surprising when Pam said, "Remember how Dad brought us here to sketch?" Their father's hobby had been painting until a third stroke had disabled him. Cathy nodded, then returned to gazing in silence. For a while, no one said anything. Then I picked up a stone and threw it into the water.

Shelley's uncle Jay smiled. "That stone took 4,000 years to wash ashore," he said. "Now you've put it back where it started."

"It wasn't a very good throw," I answered. "It'll probably only take it 2,000 years this time."

Mel smiled, too. He picked up a jagged rock and gave it his best shot. "Six thousand years, easy," he said.

Shelley heaved a heavy stone underhand.

"Two hundred years, tops." We were all smiling now. Pam gave a toss. "Aw," she said, "that'll be back by the end of the summer!"

Hours later we left the shore smoother than we had found it, having set scores of rocks back thousands of years in their quest for the shore. I wondered why their goal was to leave the ocean at all. *If it were up to me,* I thought, *I never would.* Shelley's grandpa died that week. After the funeral, we went through his things in the attic and garage. Paintings were tucked everywhere. All of them were of the ocean. There were dreamy watercolor seascapes of sky and water, oils of ships in a harbor, and pastel renderings of his girls combing the beach. He had tried to paint the ocean even after his strokes, his efforts touching and sad. I was an outsider to the family's loss, yet I was infinitely glad for having been there, having learned that the love of the ocean is the love of life, a love that never leaves us as long as we live. *We are like the rocks,* I thought, *blithely riding the tides, only to be beached until some kind hand throws us back to sea.*

*Nicole-René Rivette*

# Guided Tour

One humid day in May while walking through the New Orleans Aquarium where I worked, I heard a voice say in a heavy accent, "Excuse me, sir, can you direct me to the penguins?" I turned and found a young man in his mid-twenties accompanied by a woman in her mid-forties and an elderly woman who stood quietly behind him. The young man had a warm demeanor and stated that he had just moved to the states from South Africa. I learned that our aquarium was one of his favorites, and he had come to show his mother and grandmother our exhibits.

As it happened, my duties as an educator at the aquarium included narrating the feedings of our penguins, so I happily offered to escort them to that exhibit. As we strolled through the building I was impressed by their knowledge of ocean life. They seemed to know a great deal about many of the creatures that were housed at the aquarium. When we reached the penguin exhibit, he was pleased to see an African black-footed penguin, which was indigenous to the Cape of Good Hope, near where he grew up.

We talked about the penguins for more than an hour. The young man and his mother were very enthusiastic.

The grandmother, on the other hand, remained silent no matter how much I tried to include her in our discussions. The young man noticed this, too, because he leaned in close to me and said, "Excuse my grandmother. She is a South African woman and from a very different time when our people did not fraternize with yours." I told him that I understood why she was being that way. I remained upbeat, but I could not help but feel shaken by his admission. As a black man, I had experienced prejudice before, and it did not sting any less in this instance.

We continued to discuss the penguins, and before I knew it I had completed a full-fledged guided tour. When we reached the lobby, they thanked me vigorously, and I bid their family farewell. On the way out the door, I looked toward the grandmother one last time. She never made eye contact, nor did she allow me to do so with her.

About two months later, I came to work and found a letter in my mailbox. The letter had no name or return address. It was postmarked from South Africa and read, "Thank you for your kind tour. You are very knowledgeable, well-spoken, charming and a wonderful host. I grew up with a number of opinions on black Africans and heard even worse things about American blacks. During our visit, I watched you quietly and noticed that your love for the ocean is equal to that of my grandson. I am a very old woman and set in my ways, but you have certainly showed me that at least one of my beliefs is not true. Thank you for changing an old woman's mind."

*Nathan S. Woods*

# A Forever Ocean View

My mother and I longed for an ocean view, the kind that went on forever just like the real-estate ads boasted, where we could be swept up in the sea's changing moods. Neither of us could afford a house on the ocean, but dreaming was free so we did plenty of that. Still, we hoped someday at least one of us would realize the dream and share her good fortune with the other.

In the meantime we took every opportunity to be near the water. Each Friday we had a standing date and usually managed to fit in lunch at a seaside restaurant. We ate our way up and down the coast of Southern California, seeking new ocean-view spots to savor. We even joined a beach club because it had a great restaurant on the sand. We could lunch to the sound of waves licking the shore, watch the sea birds swoop and soar or track the progress of the California gray whale migrations. It was, we decided, the closest we would ever get to owning any part of an ocean view.

We would talk at our white-water lunches, but words weren't always necessary. Sometimes we would just watch the ocean in silence, perfectly content. Once I asked my mother about her wistful look, and she said she was imagining herself a gull flying free over the water, becoming part of the seascape. We agreed that would be a perfect way to spend time.

One Friday at the beach club, her voice broke a long comfortable silence, "Next Friday I need your help choosing my niche."

"What's a niche?" I asked.

"It's where they put people's ashes at the cemetery," she said as a wave crashed into the sand. She'd been on a mission to get her affairs in order since a recent hospitalization for congestive heart failure.

"I always thought you'd want your ashes to be spread at sea."

"Oh, no," she said, a hint of a giggle in her eyes. "You know I can't swim."

She had me laughing, breaking the somber mood that had overtaken me at the mention of cemeteries and ashes. I preferred to ignore the subject, but she was an undertaker's daughter, practical about death. She wanted to be cremated. There would be no viewing, no funeral and *no arguments*. I wasn't anxious to spend our Friday at a cemetery, but I couldn't refuse my mother.

"Where's the cemetery?" I asked, resigned to a gruesome day.

"Corona Del Mar," she said. "Pacific View Memorial Park."

*Of course,* I thought. *She was going to have her ocean view if it was the last thing she ever did.*

We met at Pacific View where the "counselor" showed us available niches. We narrowed it down to two locations in Palm Court, which resembled a giant stucco planter with marble-faced niches on all four sides and palms growing in the middle. It sat atop a hill with a panoramic view of the Pacific. That day the ocean sparkled azure blue, and Catalina Island rose up from the horizon.

One niche faced the ocean, the other looked inland. But ocean view niches are more expensive than ones looking away from the sea. Her face fell when she learned this. She probably could have afforded the view niche, but it went against her practical grain. She regrouped and began to assess the virtues of the inland niche.

"Look," she said. "It's right on the corner. You can sit here beside the niche and see the view when you visit me. I can just peek around the corner." She was teasing me again, easing the tension. "Why should I plunk out all that money to be on the view side?"

I could see she had made up her mind. She was buying the niche on the corner, without a view.

Eighteen months later she died. My sister and I placed her ashes in the niche and watched the attendant secure the marble plate with mortar. We held onto each other, eyes straining through gray haze to see the ocean our mother had loved to watch.

My Fridays were free, but I found myself at Pacific View often. Like my mother had instructed, I sat down facing the ocean. Sometimes I looked at the view, but mostly I closed my eyes and turned my head skyward. I'd see a kaleidoscope of red, yellow and orange swirls, pulling me inside the changing design and wrapping me up. It felt warm and sustaining, like a hug. When the colors subsided, I would leave, hardly glancing at the view.

After a year I was still aching and empty, crying at odd moments. A college friend came to visit, and as a lark we went to a psychic. I was stunned when she said, "Someone has recently passed on. They are worried about you and can't be free until they know you are all right."

Days later, at the niche, I thought about the psychic's words. I normally took such pronouncements lightly, but I couldn't shake this one. I sat at the niche, eyes closed as usual. I was edgy, though, and the colors faded almost as fast as they came. Hearing a bird's call, I opened my eyes to see a gull circling above. I felt the words come before I said them, "Don't worry, Mom. I'll be fine." As if in response, the gull dipped a wing, circled once more and flew off toward the ocean. My spirits lifting with the bird, I watched until it was out of sight. And there before me was that beautiful forever ocean view my mother had bought to share with me. I sat for a long time absorbing every part of it.

*Liz Zuercher*

# 3

# CELEBRATING THE BOND

*One way to open your eyes to unnoticed beauty is to ask yourself, "What if I had never seen this before? What if I knew I would never see it again?"*

Rachel Carson

# Crab Lessons

My son Geordi is a rather spirited boy. Very little holds his attention for long. He spends most of his spare time thinking up new ways to scare me half to death. Like the time he decided to "surf" on a tiny plastic lawn table that was meant to hold a few drinks rather than a six-year-old boy. Or when he came up with a new magic trick that included making his older sister disappear. Geordi had just begun learning about the ocean in school and was surprisingly fascinated by it. We lived in Delaware, so any discussion about the ocean usually included horseshoe crabs, which swarmed our coasts to mate in the late spring.

As part of the lesson, Geordi's teacher brought horseshoe crab shells to school for the children to touch and examine. When the teacher told the class that horseshoe crabs had been around for over 300 million years, even before the dinosaurs, Geordi thought that was officially the coolest thing he had ever heard. He could not stop talking about it for days, and I decided it was time for us to take a drive.

We arrived at a quiet area along the Delaware Bay. As we stepped out from the car, huge gusts of wind nearly blew my poor forty-five-pound child to the ground. Being six years old and always looking for an excuse to be goofy, Geordi saw this as an opportunity to showcase his amazing talents, which included falling down, getting up, falling down and, yes, getting up again. This, of course, was always complete with sound effects, such as, "Whoa, I'm falling . . . !" and "Help me . . . !" with giggles and snorting included. An Academy Award–winning performance as one would expect. The drama came to an abrupt halt as Geordi spied the dozens of army-truck-looking creatures in the sand. The next sound effect was "Wow!" as his body froze and his eyes widened with wonder.

Geordi ran around frantically, not knowing which one to check out first. He settled on a horseshoe crab that was on his back, legs flailing in the air. "Mom, look at this one!" he yelled. "He's cool!" I pointed out the different body parts of the crab for him, and he listened quietly and absorbed the information. Then I picked up the crab, turned it over to its proper position and placed it at the edge of the water. Geordi asked what I was doing. I explained to him that if the crab got stuck on its back and could not get back to the water soon, it would die. Horseshoe crabs, I told him, are very important in many ways. Their eggs are a great food source for birds, and their shells and blood have special medical properties that can help many people. Besides, it didn't seem right to let a species that had survived so long just shrivel up in the sun. So we watched the horseshoe crab slowly make his way back into the ocean and Geordi said, "I really liked him. I think I will name him Spike because he had all those really cool, spiky things on his back."

Geordi spotted many, many more horseshoe crabs on their backs and decided that we should help them all. Without fear or hesitation, he began picking up stranded horseshoe crabs and flipping them over, and I carried them to the water. He even assigned a name to each of them. "This one is Fuzzy, like our cat . . . this one's name will be Crazy Crab because he's moving around so much . . ." Geordi said as he flipped them over. He was extra careful and gentle, worried that he may hurt one.

When the job was done and it was time to leave, Geordi asked, "Do you think we will ever see Spike again?"

"Maybe," I said, "but now that we have helped him, we know he will be okay even if we don't see him again." Looking satisfied with that answer, Geordi said, "Yeah, that is the most important thing." And, suddenly, my son who was usually cavorting like a maniac, looked to me like a grown boy for the first time.

*Jennifer Zambri-Dickerson*

# Ebb and Flow

The sky was blue with billowing clouds. My friend Jeni and I strolled along the beach talking and enjoying the day. Unlike summer days when the sea is calm and inviting, a chilly wind had churned up the water, making it murky and far less tempting. As we gazed at the sea, Jeni pointed suddenly. "Look, Eve!" she said. A small pod of dolphins was circling just beyond the breaking waves. Next to one of the larger dolphins, a small white buoy bobbed. "I think that dolphin is caught in a line."

We both knew that being tangled would eventually kill this magnificent creature unless we could find assistance fast. We looked around the beach for someone who could help. But there was no one—it was up to us.

We entered the water and swam toward the pod. Our progress through the cold, choppy waves was slow. As we neared the pod, the dolphins moved just beyond our reach. Every time we moved closer, the dolphins moved away. It soon became clear that no matter how close we got, the dolphins would move just that much farther from us.

We treaded water, our hearts pounding, trying to think of what could be done to release the trapped dolphin. But with the dolphins continually moving away, it seemed hopeless. Suddenly, the dolphin with the "buoy" next to its head turned away from the pod. It must have sensed that we might be able to help it and began to swim directly toward us.

As the dolphin neared, it turned enough to reveal that what we thought had been a buoy was, in reality, a newborn baby dolphin that she was pushing to the surface for its first breath! We watched in awe as she pushed the baby repeatedly toward the air then turned back to her waiting pod. Slowly, as if seeing something we didn't want to believe, we noticed that the baby dolphin wasn't moving. We realized that the baby wasn't alive. All this time, the mother had tried in vain to bring it to life, to get it to behave the way she knew her newborn should behave and take that first breath that meant everything would be okay.

Not only did we not need to help, there was, indeed, nothing we could do.

Until that moment I had always distinguished humankind and the creatures of the sea in terms of "us" and "them." As I witnessed the ocean's ebb and flow—the joy of life and the grief of death—I knew we were more alike than different.

*Eve Eschner Hogan*

"Help!"

# The Friendly Isle

I met the old dockmaster by accident. I had been on vacation in Cape Cod and was taking a walk along the beach when I came across a set of footprints that led to the office of a rickety old marina. The area was littered with abandoned skiffs, their carefully printed names now obscured by barnacles and rot. Wondering who else might have interest in this dilapidated landmark, I followed the trail.

On the other side of the marina a group of teenage boys and girls was playing Wiffle ball. A boom box beside them blared loud music. They seemed to be having a good time until an old man emerged from the office of the marina. He marched toward the kids and told them they had to leave immediately.

"But where else can we play?" a boy asked.

The man glared at him. "That's not my concern. This is private property. You have to leave."

The teenagers grumbled for a minute, but seemed to respect the old man's wishes. They quickly collected their belongings and left.

Later, as I stopped to drink from the nearby water fountain, I struck up a conversation with the old man, who was scraping the remains of a frozen dinner into the sea. When I asked how he came across this place, he explained that he was the owner. He said the marina had been very successful until he had taken ill with melanoma and could no longer spend any length of time outdoors. Since then, he said, he had acquired a reputation as a hermit. I learned that the disease had struck him just a few months into his retirement. It forced him to abandon his dream of building his own vessel and sailing to the Hawaiian island of Molokai, where he had spent an unforgettable leave during his time in the U.S. Navy.

As I went on to enjoy the rest of my vacation, I could not escape the sadness of the man's tale. I wished there was something I could do. Encountering the same group of bat-toting teenagers outside the local Dairy Queen, I told them the dockmaster's story. *Maybe,* I thought, *it might discourage them from disturbing him again.* They seemed to listen, but looked unsympathetic.

I walked down that beach every morning that week. I couldn't help but wonder what it would be like to have my dreams stolen from me. No one should have to live life without something to look forward to. I decided to visit the old man again on the last day of my vacation. *Maybe some company would do him good,* I thought.

I was surprised to see the marina office open with the sound of laughter and happy chatter. One of the Wiffle ball teens greeted me at the door. She explained that the old man's story had really touched them, and they had prepared a special gift for him. The old man sat at his living-room table surrounded by half a dozen youngsters. They were all pointing at the screen of a laptop resting on the table. The old man looked up at me as I walked in, tears brimming in his eyes.

"I couldn't go to Molokai myself," he said, "so these kids brought Molokai to me."

The teens explained that, using a little bit of technology, they were able to create a "virtual tour" of Molokai, the Friendly Isle. They had painstakingly assembled a collection of breathtaking visuals and historical tidbits about the island—from the plunging waterfalls of the Halawa Valley to the thousand coconut trees of the Kapuaiwa Grove. The pièce de résistance was a striking view of the mighty Pacific from the Kalaupapa Peninsula. This peninsula, the old man explained, was where he had taken a beautiful island girl on a first date. They had carved their names on the trunk of a nearby palm.

"I haven't thought about that wonderful night in so long," the old man told them. "I never dreamed I would see it again. I can't tell you how much this means to me."

He didn't have to. It was written all over his face.

*Tal Aviezer with Jason Cocovinis*

# Dream Vacation

*I have slipped the bonds of Earth to dance with dolphins.*

Wyland

My sister Shannon stared out the window of her room at Children's Hospital. She was seventeen, tall and thin, with deep green eyes and auburn hair that was finally growing back after months of chemotherapy. Below her, passersby were bicycling, walking their dogs and jogging. She wondered aloud if they knew how fortunate they were to be outside on such a beautiful day.

She had spent most of her high-school years lying in hospitals and staring out of windows, praying for the day when her cancer would be in remission. Four years younger than me, we still shared many of the same interests. We listened to the same music, could share the same clothes and had spent weekends together boarding our friends' horses. Now, instead of sharing a bedroom, I kept Shannon company by spending nights on a reclining chair in her hospital room.

"Oh well," she told me, "at least they gave me a nice room this time."

This was true. Shannon had a private room at the back of the hospital with a large, room-length window that overlooked Audubon Park. To the left she could watch the sun glisten off the Mississippi River. Tired from standing, she wheeled her IV stand back to her hospital bed. A nurse brought in a tray of food. I got up, hoping to remove the tray before the smell of the food could reach Shannon's nose. Too late. Even though she was finished with her chemotherapy, the smell of food still nauseated her.

The tray was the last straw.

"I'm tired of being trapped in this hospital!" she said. "I feel like I'm in prison."

"Don't worry," I said. "When they finish these last few tests, they promised to let you out on good behavior." That was all I needed to change the subject to the trip to Key West we had been planning for weeks. This was to be her "remission" vacation, a trip that was going to take her far away from all this and connect her back to the outside world.

When "remission" day did come, our parents, Shannon, our little brother Jason and I piled into a Jeep for the long drive to the coast. On the way, we talked about how Shannon would now be able to graduate with her class since she had been taking school courses at home and what college she would attend so she could study marine biology. We sang our favorite Disney songs from *The Little Mermaid* . . . and before we knew it we were in the Florida Keys.

There was just one thing on our itinerary—Shannon's dream to swim with dolphins. As we entered the Keys, a large wall mural of a mermaid surrounded by her underwater friends welcomed us. Shannon pointed and said, "That will be us tomorrow!"

As we drove over the bridges to Key West, we strained to catch a glimpse of dolphins playing in the gulf. Later, after checking into our hotel, we rounded up a phone book and reserved a dolphin excursion for the next morning. Shannon's dream was finally going to come true!

The next morning at the marina, we boarded a catamaran that had been airbrushed with pictures of dolphins playing at sunset. As the boat pulled out from the dock, our captain played the "Winnie the Pooh" song to set the pace for a carefree day.

We arrived at an area of shallow water referred to as a "playground" for the dolphins. The captain asked, "Who wants to swim in the water first?" Shannon, of course, volunteered. She had waited too long not to jump in at the first opportunity. Nearly as excited as she was, I decided to join her. Soon the water was bubbling with commotion. Attracted by our presence, a pod of dolphins flipped and danced beneath us. Clicks and chirps, almost like laughter, were everywhere. It was like nothing we had ever heard! The energy the dolphins projected only intensified our enthusiasm.

We had brought underwater cameras with the intention of taking a few snapshots. But as the dolphins rushed past us, always an arm's length away, we quickly forgot about taking pictures. For hours, we took turns in the water, two at a time, swimming and snorkeling. The dolphins never seemed to tire. Neither did Shannon. Even underwater, I could see the look of total exhilaration on her face as one dolphin after another gracefully glided by. This was her dream. And it had become more real than she could have ever possibly imagined.

When the captain announced it was time to leave, we reluctantly boarded the boat. As we headed back, the dolphins continued to follow us, playing and jumping in the waves as if they were bidding us good-bye. Later that evening as we sat at the dock at Mallory Square and watched the sunset fade, I saw something wonderful in

Shannon's eyes. It reminded me of the carefree spirit of the dolphins that we had seen earlier. Shannon was at ease.

Four months later, her cancer relapsed. This time her body was unable to fight off the disease due to her already weakened system. In April, she passed away. It is comforting to know that I got to experience with Shannon the fulfillment of at least one of her dreams. If only for a brief period, she truly was living her life how she wanted to. Free.

*Jennifer Lowry*

# Letters

My earliest memories are of my mother and me at the beach in Florida, playing in the ocean. She would stand at the water's edge and explain that a beach very much like ours was just over the horizon, bordering the same ocean. Her point was that although we couldn't see the other side, the ocean still connected us to the people who lived there.

On my first day of school I stood at the classroom door, my heart beating wildly, and told my mom I didn't want to stay. I wanted to go to the beach with her instead.

"We can go after school," she said.

"But I'll miss you," I cried. "I don't want you to go away."

Understanding my fear, she repeated the one thing that always soothed me. She pointed to the picture of the globe that decorated my lunchbox and said, "No matter where we are, we'll always be connected by the ocean." I stared at the ocean picture, salty water in my blue eyes. Dutifully, I nodded, then turned and walked through the door.

Years later I joined the U.S. Navy. I was at sea for six months at a time. My mother and I exchanged letters, but the delivery delays made it hard to keep any kind of continuing thread in our correspondence. So we developed a game for our letters. We would pick a day to write about and try to guess what the other one was doing or wearing that day. To our surprise we were incredibly accurate with our predictions. My mother soon discovered hers were even more accurate when she meditated and wrote at the ocean's edge, her feet in the water where we used to play—the same water I was sailing half a globe away.

In May 1987, I was onboard the USS *Doyle* in the Persian Gulf—my last six-month voyage before I would be honorably discharged from the navy. By this time my mother and I had decided to change our letter game. Since the mail delivery was taking about a month, we agreed to write at the same time and day (taking into account the time difference) and try to predict a month ahead what the other was doing and feeling.

The helicopter carrying our mail arrived on May 17, the very day my mother and I had chosen to write about, and I was more excited than usual to read her letter. I always looked forward to her letters. They were always so upbeat they helped me get through the month. But I was especially curious to see if our predictions would still be so accurate. Since I had to be on watch shortly, I read as I walked to the combat information center. She wrote:

*Dear Michael,*

*I went down to the ocean where we played when you were a child. I walked into the water and began to meditate about the day we agreed upon. I looked at the ocean's horizon and thought of you and how the ocean connects us. I thought long and hard about writing this as it might make you sad, but as I stood in the water I saw you as a child with your lunchbox, crying as you turned and walked through the door at school so many years ago. I went to the beach that day after dropping you off and cried. Now, there I was back doing the same thing. All I felt was sadness, and when a plane flew by overhead I got scared. For the first time in my life, I felt afraid of being in the water. I couldn't even come up with a single prediction to give you. I'm sorry that our experiment didn't work.*

I was a little shocked and confused at the gloomy tone of her letter. I had reached the radar room, and in order to open the door I juggled the letter and the box of food I carried with me for my twelve-hour shift. As I crossed the threshold carrying my "lunch box," a strong sense of déjà vu hit me, and I could not help thinking about the irony as I sat down at the air search radar. With my mother's words echoing in my mind, I began my watch. I could feel the ocean move under my feet and hear the water sliding by the steel grey hull of the ship. Always a comfort before, the water now seemed ominous.

Every aircraft that flew near our ship that day left me feeling anxious. I even challenged a regular commercial aircraft, which quickly veered off. Moments later the USS *Stark*, our sister ship a few short nautical miles away, failed to challenge the same commercial aircraft and was struck from overhead by two Iraqi aircraft-fired Exocet missiles. Thirty-seven shipmates were killed, and the *Stark* nearly sank.

Although I can't say for certain that my mother's letter saved my shipmates and me that day, I do know that what she wrote made me more vigilant. I felt like she and I were held together somehow, bound across the globe by the waters lapping at her feet and licking the hull of my ship. I don't think our experiment could have worked any better.

*Michael Geers*

# Goddess

I recently took my oldest daughter Maya to our local beach to swim and play. She's four years old, and naturally her questions have become more thoughtful and profound. At the beach she asked—without any prompting from me—"God made us, huh?" We had been working on a sand castle when she said this. I smoothed away loose sand from our castle and took a deep breath, frightened, really, to mess up this answer .

I considered myself spiritual, but by no means religious. I believe in compassion, giving your all and doing right by yourself, others and the Earth. The religious symbolism I allow in our house is defined by our Afro-Caribbean culture. I have a shelf—some call it an altar—covered with candles, pictures of saints, shells, a coconut, coins, feathers and beaded necklaces. These things are important definers of who we were as Puerto Ricans, but for the most part they have remained a mystery to Maya. Now she is getting old enough to ask for some explanation.

Before she lost interest, I said, finally, "Yes, Baby, God made us."

That was all I could come up with—a simple answer to a simple question.

"How did she do that?"

*She?* I thought. "Well," I said, "there are a lot of stories about how she did that. Some say she molded people out of the Earth and breathed life into them. And some say that a long, long time ago before dinosaurs were around she made tiny animals first that eventually turned into people."

"Turned into people?"

"After a really long time, yeah, the animals *evolved* into people." Impressively, I knew she understood that word because she once told me that Pokémon evolve.

"Will Puffy [our cat] evolve into a person?"

"Probably not," I laughed. "It takes a really long time if that were to ever happen again."

"Is God a boy or a girl?"

"I think God is both, Baby."

"Spencer says God is a boy!" She said this with a tone revealing the audacity of Spencer, one of her classmates. I tried to imagine preschoolers discussing religion on the monkey bars or around the water fountain.

"It's okay that Spencer thinks that," I said.

"Oh," she answered, sounding a bit defeated that maybe Spencer had won a minor victory.

"I think," I said gingerly, "that God is, and looks like, all things in nature."

"Everything?"

"Sure. The sun, the flowers, plants." I pointed to the water. "The ocean." Her eyes followed my hand. "Some say that the ocean is a girl god." Her face brightened. I was offering her the first introduction to a religion that our great-great-grandparents most likely practiced with great passion, as if their identity depended on it. I was proud and scared, praying I would present it right.

"Her name is Yemaya," I said.

"Maya?" she giggled.

"YE-ma-YA," I said again.

Maya seemed pleased. She looked at the ocean again. A small wave broke and rolled. Slowly, it spread a thin layer of water over the dark sand. "Yemaya," she repeated.

"Yemaya is a goddess. That's what they call a girl god. She's the goddess of the ocean that is part of a bigger God that made us. She is strong and beautiful. She takes care of a lot of people, but sometimes she can destroy things, too."

I watched Maya's face, wondering how she was processing this story. I wanted to believe that it hit her someplace where spirituality and myth are the same. Then my beautiful, bright, yet still four-year-old asked, "Do you think Yemaya likes to wear pink dresses?"

I laughed again.

"I think maybe white and blue dresses," I said. "They say she likes those colors."

"Not pink? How about purple?"

"Maybe purple." What was I going to say, that Yemaya doesn't like purple?

"Mami?" I thought for sure Maya would go on to ask about every color dress and whether Yemaya liked them or not, but instead she said quietly, "If God looks like Yemaya, can God even look like me?"

I tried to remember something Maya Angelou had once said—after all I had named Maya after her—about the power and importance of the ocean. I couldn't remember the exact quote because all that overcame me was that Maya, my Maya, was just as powerful and important as the ocean to me. And I said to her, wiping salty water from my face, "Yes, baby, certainly God looks like you, too."

*Danette Rivera*

# The Guide

Many years ago, my dad and I were driving back to my home on the north shore of Oahu when we noticed a large white albatross tied to a small fruit stand next to the Kamehameha Highway. Near the bird stood a local Tongan man. I pulled to the side of the road and asked the man what he thought he was doing. "These birds are protected in Hawaii," I said. "Did you know that?"

The man didn't seem to care. He said the bird helped to draw tourists. To him, it was nothing more than a photo opportunity for anyone who drove by. I did my best to convince him this was wrong, how the albatross was a wild animal that depended on access to the sea for food. To a bird that is capable of flying hundreds of miles in a day, I could imagine no worse torture than being lashed to a structure on the side of a road.

After an hour of negotiation, the man reluctantly released the bird to me. In turn, I handed it over to my neighbor, a local expert known around the North Shore as the bird lady. She agreed to care for the albatross until it could recover enough for release back into the wild.

After a few days, the albatross looked healthier and seemed strong enough to fly. We had done all we could;

the rest was up to the bird. We took it to the beach at Kewela Bay, where it tried several times to take off. After the third try, it caught a gust of wind, and with a beat of its wings, took to the air. As clumsy as they are on land, there is nothing more beautiful than the sight of a soaring albatross, and I have to admit we were all moved at the sight of this bird returning to the wild. It quickly gained altitude, and just when we thought we had seen the last of it, it banked suddenly, and in a graceful turn, swept over our heads in what I liked to think of as a final good-bye.

* * *

Ten years later, I was scheduled to return to the mainland for a series of gallery shows. As I made my preparations to leave, I had to move my small zodiac boat from its mooring in front of my house to Haleiwa harbor. My friend Gary offered to drive my pick-up truck with the boat trailer to the boat ramp in Haleiwa, while I drove the boat to meet him a half-hour later. Gary left with the trailer, and I waded out to the boat to get started.

My timing couldn't have been worse. A winter swell was growing offshore. The waves seemed manageable at first, but within minutes I was battling enormous swells. The boat was hammered from every direction. Turning back would have been useless, not to mention even more dangerous. My only option was to race for the horizon and hope for the best. I gunned the engine toward the outer reefs, but the swells kept coming, as if God had grabbed the ocean like a blanket and was shaking it violently.

The North Shore is known for some of the largest waves in the world, and this was as big as I'd seen it in twenty years. To make matters worse, I had forgotten to bring a life preserver. If a wave washed me from the boat, I was done for. Wave after wave pounded the boat, each wave getting bigger, and each time the boat seemed to barely make it over. I had lost all sense of direction and began to consider the very real possibility of getting killed, when out of nowhere a great albatross swooped past the bow of the boat, its great wings dipping from side to side as it latched onto a current of air less than twenty feet in front of me.

The bird soared between the swells, navigating toward an area of calm. I, too, felt a sudden calm come over me. The fact that I was no longer alone filled me with the hope that I might survive this after all. All I could do was put my trust in the bird's instincts and its knowledge of the unforgiving sea. For two hours, the amazing bird not only stayed with me, but actually led me into the safe harbor, then banked gently and turned toward the horizon until it disappeared from sight.

*Wyland*

# Octopus's Garden

*We cannot have peace among men whose hearts find delight in killing any living creature.*
Rachel Carson

When I moved to Maui to marry the Captain of my heart, one of the marriage requirements was that I learn to scuba dive—as that was his first love. If I were to fit in, this ocean of his and I were just going to have to get along! Luckily for me—and us—I already had an ongoing love affair with the sea, both for its beauty and its creatures, so I embraced this opportunity to dive and explore the world below the surface.

There were a few differences between the way my fiancé and I approached the sea, however. Having been a fisherman for many years, he didn't think twice about taking the ocean's bounty home for dinner. In fact, he had told me how the Hawaiians had taught him to kill an octopus by biting it right between the eyes, then taking it home to eat. Useful information, I'm sure, but all it did for me was offer proof that the worst gift one could have was to be born delicious.

I, on the other hand, had been a vegetarian for over twenty years. I wasn't the kind of vegetarian who concerned herself with what other people ate, but I preferred, when given the option, not to participate in or witness the death of any creature.

One day, when we were exploring the waters off the coast of Maui, we happened across an octopus's garden. Romantically, the Beatles' song of the same name started playing in my head. The Captain had different tunes playing in his head, and they must have sounded like dinner bells, because after catching the octopus and showing me its spectacular array of arms and suction cups, he paused. I could see on his face that this was a very difficult moment.

As he held the octopus, visions of the Captain biting the head of this multiarmed creature flashed through my mind. I imagined the arms—now so full of life and movement— falling limp at the hands of my beloved. My emotions must have shown in my eyes, the only part of my face visible behind mask, regulator and a steady stream of bubbles.

Still holding the giant octopus in his hands as it reached out in every direction to get away, the Captain looked at me, then looked at the octopus. He was obviously in the grip of one of the major decisions of his life: Did he want to take the octopus home for dinner or take the girl home for life? He must have realized that this could be the deal breaker and, ever so reluctantly, he opened his hand and let the octopus go. As they parted each other's company, it was clear that the octopus and the Captain both celebrated their new lease on life.

Evidently, the Captain never forgot the moment, either. On our ten-year wedding anniversary, he graced me with a beautiful, silver necklace of an eight-armed beauty of the sea in honor of the octopus that saved our relationship.

*Eve Eschner Hogan*

# I Found a Tiny Starfish

I found a tiny starfish
In a tide pool by the sand.
I found a tiny starfish
And put him in my hand.

An itty-bitty starfish
No bigger than my thumb,
A wet and golden starfish
Belonging to no one.

I thought that I would take him
From the tide pool by the sea,
And bring him home to give to you
A loving gift from me.

But as I held my starfish,
His skin began to dry.
Without his special seaside home,
My gift to you would die.

I found a tiny starfish
In a tide pool by the sea.
I hope whoever finds him next
Will leave him there, like me!

And the gift I've saved for you?
The best gift I can give:
I found a tiny starfish,
And for you, I let him live.

*Dayle Ann Dodds*
*Submitted by Courtenay Mayes, age 12*

# After the Beach

We were traveling as we often do on Sundays, looking for places for the children to play, when we found a beautiful, abandoned stretch of beach. The day was glorious. I brought a book, a novel about castles and kings, so that I might sit and read in my "matureness" while the children frolicked like untethered colts. But this time something in their playfulness stirred me to put the book down.

I moved closer to see what they were up to. My eldest daughter was building her own castle close to the water line and calling it the Taj Mahal. She moved giant buckets of sand to build it higher, and I laughed at her vain attempts to get the family dog employed in digging at just the right spot. My youngest daughter asked if I wanted to join her and, like an excited new friend, I quickly agreed. We worked on a piece of monolithic proportion. I likened it to a lost Mayan temple, but she wanted it to be the home of a magical princess called Leah, who hid in the far sand tower and could only be seen by her.

As the sun set, we gave our castles a rest and enjoyed the last hours of a fragrant summer day, until the sudden oncoming tide sent us back to building. My youngest tried to complete the tunnel outside her temple before the ocean struck. But it was too late. The water was upon us and, with dusk approaching, we gave up. The time to leave had arrived. The children moaned and asked to stay a little longer. Their father was firm in his plans to leave until I protested a little, too. So we lingered there on our little stretch of beach and watched the waves roll for a few moments more.

We talked about getting a better contractor for the next family sand mansion and which of the five remaining towers the princess might be hiding in. We whooped and aahed as the ocean waves crept over our Taj Mahal. We marveled at a power much greater than ourselves that moved the tides on this planet and in our lives. I explained that these were the tides that brought Father from faraway England and Mother's ancestors, full of faith and hope, to this new land long ago.

A few tourists passed, but I no longer worried about my appearance. I imagined the adults looking longingly as they saw my sandy arms and legs. I bet they secretly wished they had a child within them that would help them build pyres to the sun, castles of invisible princesses and sacrifices to the waves. We watched as the whole kingdom was swallowed and returned to the sand, to await the dreams of another builder, another time. My youngest brought home a bucket of sand where the princess was hiding. "She's going to live under our rosebushes from now on," she said.

We stopped for ice cream on the way home. The man at the store remarked how young I looked, but it's what I felt that was so delicious: young again and full of wonder. The next morning, taking my coffee out on our sun deck, I nearly tripped over a tiny pair of sandy shoes. It should have annoyed me, but it didn't. My bones may have ached, but I was happy. As I watched the sun rise, my husband joined me. "I creak," I said to him. He shook his head.

"No," he said softly, touching my sunburned nose, "you glow, my little sand queen. You glow."

*Nancy V. Bennett*

# Sea Dog

It was in the busy industrial seaport of Kaohsiung, Taiwan, that Chung Chin-Po, captain of the oil tanker *Insiko* 1907, received an unexpected gift from a friend: a two-week-old terrier puppy to accompany him on his long voyages. Honored, the captain named the puppy Hok-Get, a Taiwanese word meaning happiness, blessings and good fortune—qualities he hoped the little dog might somehow bestow upon the *Insiko* and its crew.

It soon seemed that the captain was right. Life at sea could be very lonely, and for the next two years the frisky little dog provided a happy diversion and faithful companionship for the ship's crew. She scampered about the constantly rolling ship and was soon traversing the stairwells and gangways from the bridge down to the engine room. She learned where to hide below deck when the swells churned, and when the weather was calm she went above deck to chase seagulls and take afternoon naps. It seemed that things couldn't have gotten any better aboard the *Insiko*.

Then, as the ship crossed the South Pacific, a fire swept through the *Insiko*, killing one crewman, injuring another and gutting the entire engine room. All power and communications were lost. The ship was at the mercy of the currents. For twenty-one days, Chin-Po and his crew huddled on the deck searching for passing vessels, until a passing cruise ship, the *Norwegian Star,* spotted them and transferred the starving crew to safety.

But the rescue ship had overlooked one member of *Insiko* during the confusion of the rough-seas transfer— the little dog, Hok-Get. By the time Captain Chi-Po and the others realized the mistake, it was too late to turn back. Hok-Get had been abandoned to the fate of the sea. Her prospects for survival were grim and might have been even worse had it not been for a tourist aboard the *Norwegian Star* who later reported the faint barking of a dog as the ship pulled away from the crippled *Insiko.*

The next day, when the *Norwegian Star* stopped in Lahaina, Maui, the story of the little dog left behind found its way into the media spotlight. Flooded by donations from the public, the Hawaiian Humane Society launched a $50,000 effort to rescue Hok-Get. The air-and-sea search spanned three days and covered 14,800 square miles, but with no sign of the vessel, the *Insiko* was presumed sunk, and the rescue effort was called off. The Humane Society declared Hok-Get lost at sea.

A week later, the fishing vessel *Victoria City* made radar contact with an unidentified ship about 400 nautical miles south of the island of Kauai. The description to the Coast Guard of "a darkened ship with no lights that appeared to be adrift" matched that of *Insiko.* Once again the Humane Society was bombarded by requests and donations from animal lovers from the United States, South Africa, Great Britain, Canada and Brazil. The search to find the *Insiko* and Hok-Get was resumed. Once again the rescue teams were unable to relocate the drifting vessel.

Then, by chance, a Coast Guard search-and-rescue plane spotted a ship drifting 260 miles east of Johnston

Island atoll. As the plane moved closer, the pilot spotted a little white dog running frantically back and forth across the deck of the bridge wing. The crew collected pizza and granola bars from their box lunches, placed them in an empty sonar buoy and, with some careful maneuvering, managed to drop the food onto the deck.

Aerial images of the excited little dog running across the deck of the burned-out tanker were broadcast worldwide. A week later, a tugboat called *American Quest* reached the *Insiko*. The tugboat had been called on to keep the *Insiko* from drifting onto a nearby ecological preserve, where it threatened to run aground and spill more than 60,000 gallons of diesel fuel. The rescue crew found Hok-Get, starved and frightened from her twenty-five-day odyssey at sea, hiding under a pile of tires near the bow of the ship. The lonely and fearful chapter of her life aboard the *Insiko* had finally come to an end.

When the *American Quest*, with *Insiko* in tow, finally docked at Pier 24 of Honolulu Harbor, Hok-Get emerged in the arms of a rescuer to a red-carpet welcome of supporters and media from around the world. Her tail wagging and a bright red flower lei around her neck, Hok-Get was the picture of happiness, blessings and good fortune that captain Chin-Po had foretold. The little dog had brought out the generosity and compassion of the world with her resilience and spirit, proving that every life, no matter how small, deserves to be cherished.

*Jon L. Rishi*

# What Do You See?

Gary loved his job at the Aquarium of the Pacific in Long Beach, California. He was an onstage presenter and narrated the wondrous exhibits in some of the largest and most interesting habitats in the aquarium. One day in July, he was speaking to a large group of guests about the Tropical Pacific exhibit. The exhibit, made to look like an exotic lagoon, was home to thousands of brilliantly colored fish from the coral shores of the islands of Palau. Gary's voice, as always, was soothing and pleasant. He welcomed visitors to a habitat that contained, ". . . three hundred and fifty thoooouuusand gallons of real sea water. The water this afternoon is a balmy seventy-eight degrees . . . just as these magnificent creatures like it."

With poetic detail, he described the beautiful swimming patterns of the zebra sharks and the black-tipped reef sharks. He pointed out a male and female Napoleon wrasse and noted, "Just look at him with those gorgeous big ol' blue lips and her with the fiery peachy-yellow ones. What a *lovely* couple!" He talked about the porcupine fish and the strange defensive habits of the puffer family to which it belonged, then segued into a description of the trigger family of fishes and the humu humu nuku nuku apuaa of Hawaii.

A pretty young lady in her twenties had been standing next to Gary. She seemed to be hanging on his every word. Midway through the presentation, the woman leaned over and said to Gary, "I love listening to your voice. When you talk, I can picture the animals swimming around and moving through the coral." Gary usually asked guests to hold comments until the end of the show, but the haunting manner of the woman seemed to catch him off guard. She was pretty, intelligent and seemed exceptionally interested in marine life. "I could listen to you forever," the woman said. Gary was flattered. He thanked the woman for such a nice compliment, then went back to work.

After the presentation, Gary was answering questions about the exhibit when a man approached him. The man was full of compliments, too. He thanked Gary for such a beautiful presentation and asked him a couple of questions regarding the fish. Then he asked if Gary noticed anything unusual about the young lady who was talking with him a few moments ago. Gary said he did not. "That's okay," the man said. "A lot of people don't notice. She's my granddaughter—and she's blind."

*Gary Riedel*

*Dolphin Seas*

*Original painting by Wyland* ©2003.

# 4

# OCEAN WISDOM

*All is born of water; all is sustained by water.*

*Goethe*

# A Lesson from the Sea

Until I was fourteen I had never been far from my father's farm. And because the only water close by was in ponds, the river and a small lake, I could scarcely imagine what a vast sea must be like. People said that sometimes when the wind came from the west, the fields of young wheat looked like waves, but I don't think anyone where I lived knew what an ocean wave looked like.

Then my Aunt Harriet and Uncle Ted invited me to spend two weeks with them in Spring Lake, New Jersey. They had taken a house there for the summer and thought I would enjoy the shore.

I guess I'd become something of a trial at home because I had more attitude adjustments from my dad that year than you'd believe—maybe one of the reasons my parents so readily agreed to let me go away.

Before I knew it, I was standing on a wide beach looking at the great Atlantic Ocean for the first time in my life. I'd been so eager to see it that I talked my uncle into walking the short block to the beach before I was even unpacked.

It was not what I expected. The waves were easy and gentle, more like a lake, I thought. But the horizon seemed very far away and the air sure didn't smell like Indiana.

Just breathing made me feel a little light-headed and happy. "It's just like a big lake," I said.

"It's quiet today," my uncle said. "The ocean has many moods, though. This is just one of them." I heard an odd kind of respect in his voice that I did not understand.

I waded into the water up to the limits of my rolled-up jeans and picked up a bright blue piece of glass. It was frosted and very smooth. My uncle told me that the sea and sand did that. "Powerful forces," he said. "I don't want you in the water without one of us with you."

"I can swim," I said, more to ease his concern than to brag. "Mom says I loved the water from the day I was born."

"Most people who drown can swim and love the water," he said. "Let's go to the house, get you unpacked, have some lunch, and then we can come down to the beach in the afternoon and get you initiated."

We did that. I don't think many things in my life have been as much fun as swimming in the Atlantic summer surf. Day after day, the sky was clear, the waves easy, the water just warm enough. I was at the beach as soon as I could get an adult to go with me and stayed long after they were ready to go back to the house. Before long I met three guys my own age, and we began to hang out almost every day to body surf.

In the evenings I sat on the porch with my aunt and uncle and drank iced tea or lemonade. Sometimes we sang the kind of old songs you sing in summer camp. Sometimes we took a drive to Atlantic City to see the boardwalk. But mostly it was the ocean that had my attention. My uncle had rented a small star-class skiff and began to teach me how to sail it.

I was a natural, he soon said. "You have a real feel for it. And you learn fast. I only have to tell you once and you've got it." After a day at the beach, on or in the water, I went to sleep every night listening to the steady, reassuring sound of the surf. I thought of the ocean as my friend and the source of more fun than I'd ever known.

Then one morning I awoke to a dull, gray sky and a noise I'd never heard before. I walked to the end of our street as soon as I got up. The sea was just beyond a low retaining wall, and it looked much more exciting than I'd ever seen it. The waves were big and dark, and the white-caps were dazzling. I could see three boys I'd met on the town beach already in the water. They were laughing and screaming when a large wave overtook them. They body surfed all the way into the shore. It looked like it was going to be a great day.

At breakfast I asked, first thing, when we could go to the beach. My uncle had some things to do and said we would go in about an hour. I asked if I could go ahead because my friends were already in the water.

"You better wait for me this time," my uncle said. "I won't be long. The sea is a little high today. You'll have to be careful."

"Okay," I said. "I'll go down and get some sun and wait for you."

"Lots of screen," he said. "You can burn even under those clouds. And do not—I repeat—do not go in the water."

Of course, the ocean was irresistible. I knew it as my friend. I'd had the best time of my life sailing on it, swimming in it, dodging its waves, feeling the strength of it lift my body high on the swell. I tried to wait for my uncle, but the pull of the sea was too much for me and I went in to join my friends.

We were all excited and constantly looking for the seventh wave, which we all imagined to be bigger than the rest. The trouble, of course, was where did you begin to count? So we picked the largest wave in a course and counted from there. In about a half an hour we got it right and waded on wave six as far out as we dared go to catch wave seven.

And then it came. It seemed larger than anything I'd ever seen, rolling at us from across the great expanse of ocean. It rolled and threatened to cap and then just kept coming on. We all pointed at it, shouted at each other and got ready to either ride or duck it. I think I was still thinking about which to do when it hit.

I had turned broadside to it, and the great wave picked me up and tossed me on its crest like a cork. I bounced for what seemed a very long time, and then it threw me into its trough and pulled me under the water. I hit the sand bottom with my back, was rolled over and over, turned this way and that. Even though I had to get some air in the next few seconds, I could not tell which way was up. I forced my body toward the light. I broached the surface, gulped air and was once again pulled under and pounded down into the sand. The green water roiled around me, rolling and tossing me as though I were a pebble. I believed I was about to take the last breath I'd ever take.

My life did not flash before me, as people say it does, but my feelings did. I remembered countless joys at home that were more intense than I knew they were at the time. How I felt rolling in a raked pile of leaves, how the warm water of our pond felt on my skin, how my mother looked at me when she put a plate of chocolate chip cookies on the table, how my father could not suppress his pride when I won a horse show. Small, ordinary things of great joy filled my mind, and I tried to turn my head once again toward the light.

But the sea seemed determined to keep me pinned to the sand like a wrestler trying for a win. I didn't have strength left to fight it, and the moment I gave up, the sea picked me up once more and spit me out in shallow water.

My friends came and helped drag me out onto the sand. I sat dazed and sputtering, trying to catch my breath while they all talked about what a great ride it had been. Not for me. I finally began to breathe a little easier when I opened my eyes and saw the legs of a man in white twill pants. I followed them to the man's face and immediately lowered my head, waiting for the lecture. It did not come.

And it never did. My uncle walked me home. We had lunch and went sailing in the afternoon after the sea had quieted. He never once mentioned my having disobeyed him.

Some years later, after my college commencement ceremony, my family had the usual send-the-kid-out-into-the-world dinner. At one point we began to talk about the most important lessons we each had managed to learn. I remembered that day at the beach when my uncle stood over me on the sand as I tried to get my breath and said nothing. I asked him why he had done that, and he said, "I didn't know whether to hug you or kick you in the butt, so silence seemed to be the best option. Besides, the sea is the finest teacher there is. I could see that you had learned what you needed to know."

He was right about that. I've loved the sea all my life and have spent many days sailing or walking beaches. But since that amazing day when the sea became my teacher I've respected it even more than loved it. It is, indeed, a powerful teacher. I looked at my family seated around that table and thought how good it was to be alive, to be with them and to have had once in my youth such an unforgettable and forgiving teacher.

*Walker Meade*

# A Prayer for the Ocean

*To stand at the edge of the sea . . . is to have knowledge of things that are as eternal as any earthly life can be.*

Rachel Carson
*Under the Sea-Wind*

My life's passion for knowing and feeling the peace of God led me to live on Maui. Somehow, the sacredness of this vast expanse of blue inspires me more here than any other place on Earth. In awe, I contemplate the creator's hand each day in the immense waters surrounding me; in the whales and their babies, with their mystical songs; in the dolphins and their gentle playfulness; in the magnificent, changing kaleidoscope of reef fish, starfish and turtles; in the infinite canvas of creativity beneath this water. My heart expands when I contemplate the mystery, continuity and tranquility I'm offered by the sea.

Its lessons are eternal.

The ocean reminds me to be fluid and flow with life. It helps me to remember that everything has a rhythm and to respect those cycles. It inspires me to shine like the sunlight that dances across the water and to reflect as the moon and stars do on a quiet night. To remember that life is as the ocean itself, ever-changing, and to understand that I cannot control everything. It reminds me to deeply breathe in the new and exhale the old with love, much as the tides ebb and flow. To appreciate beauty, even in a storm, and to rise above the turbulence.

The ocean has been my greatest teacher, and daily I give thanks for the insights and serenity it has provided. Daily I pray that the world will protect and respect this sacred, God-given resource so it may continue to inspire, heal and bless those who come after us on this beautiful planet.

*Wyland*

# The Perfect Shell

*I seem to have been like a child playing on the seashore, finding now and then a prettier shell than ordinary, whilst the great ocean of truth lay undiscovered before me.*

Isaac Newton

When I was three years old, my parents took me to the beach for the first time. I remember how quickly I fell in love with the smell of the salty air, the roar of the crashing waves on the shore and the feeling of wet sand between my toes. I was fascinated by all of the different shells, pebbles and stones embedded in the sand. It was then that I began my hobby of collecting seashells, always on the lookout for something new and strange, always amazed at how unique each one was.

After three years, my collection was quite impressive. I had clamshells, some mussels, a scallop shell here and there—all equally amazing to a six-year-old. One day, I was standing at the beach feeling the cool water run over my feet when the biggest, most beautiful conch shell I had ever seen rolled in with the tide. It was one of those shells that held the sound of the ocean, and the reflection from the sun made it glow bright shades of pink and ivory. The shell was perfect. I reached down and, for an instant, felt the smooth exterior brush against my fingertips. My heart pounded in awe at such a discovery. Suddenly, the tide crashed in, tore the shell from my grasp and sent it hurtling back into the sea. I stood there, stunned, confused over what had just happened. I couldn't bear to move. *Maybe it will come back,* I thought. *Maybe if I just wait a while, if I am patient, it will return.* I sat down in the wet sand, letting the tide rush over me, barely noticing the salty water through my tears.

The shell never did return, and I have now spent my life searching for it. It seems to be a theme in my life, I have always thought, this shell escaping. Always coming so close to perfection and having the object of my desire snatched away from me at the last second. The parallel between my lost shell and so many events in my life has been an unsettling mystery. I have spent years looking for what might have been. Hundreds of hours staring into the ocean waiting for the answers to rush over me in the salt-tinged wind. Searching with nothing to show for it but a long, depressing string of broken relationships, missed opportunities and lost loved ones. Isn't that the story of all of our lives, though? We are always looking for that perfect mate, the perfect job or the perfect situation to grace us with its presence, but it never does. Does it really exist, after all?

I am almost thirty years old now, and I still collect seashells. My husband and I take our children to the beach as often as possible, and I have tried to share my love of the ocean with them. My daughter has developed an affinity for collecting shells and stones. When she was six years old, she made an amazing discovery, too. I saw her running toward me, sand flying in all directions, hands waving in the air, smiling the brightest smile imaginable.

In her right hand was a small, dull and raggedy, ivory-colored and rather ordinary-looking clamshell. Slightly out of breath, she stopped before me and declared in a loud, excited voice, "Mommy, I have found the most beautiful shell in the world for you! It's perfect!" I felt the tears begin to well in my eyes as I looked at her and realized that this was the perfect shell. It was the one I had spent my entire life looking for because it was given with perfect love. The perfection I sought had been there all the time. I just needed to know where to look.

*Jennifer Zambri-Dickerson*

•

# The Day at the Beach

*After a visit to the beach, it's hard to believe that we live in a material world.*

Pam Shaw

Not long ago, I came to one of those bleak periods that many of us encounter from time to time, a sudden drastic dip in the graph of living when everything goes stale and flat, energy wanes, enthusiasm dies. The effect on my work was frightening. Every morning I clenched my teeth and muttered: "Today life will take on some of its old meaning. You've got to break through this thing. You've got to."

But the barren days dragged on, and the paralysis grew worse. The time came when I knew I needed help.

The man I turned to was a doctor. Not a psychiatrist, just a doctor. He was older than I, and under his surface gruffness lay great wisdom and experience. "I don't know what's wrong," I told him miserably, "but I just seem to have come to a dead end. Can you help me?"

"I don't know," he said slowly. He made a tent of his fingers and gazed at me thoughtfully for a long while. Then, abruptly, he asked, "Where were you happiest as a child?"

"As a child?" I echoed. "At the beach, I suppose. We had a summer cottage there. We all loved it."

He looked out the window and watched the October leaves sifting down. "Are you capable of following instructions for a single day?"

"I think so," I said, ready to try anything.

"All right. Here's what I want you to do."

He told me to drive to the beach alone the following morning, arriving not later than nine o'clock. I could take some lunch, but I was not to read, write, listen to the radio or talk to anyone. "In addition," he said, "I'll give you a prescription to be taken every three hours."

He tore off four prescription blanks, wrote a few words on each, folded them, numbered them and handed them to me. "Take these at nine, twelve, three and six."

"Are you serious?" I asked.

He gave me a short honk of laughter. "You won't think I'm joking when you get my bill!"

The next morning, with little faith, I drove to the beach. It was lonely, all right. A northeaster was blowing; the sea looked gray and angry. I sat in the car, the whole day stretching emptily before me. Then I took out the first of the folded slips of paper. On it was written: *Listen carefully.*

I stared at the two words. I thought, *The man must be crazy.* He had ruled out music and newscasts and human conversation. What else was there?

I raised my head and listened. There were no sounds but the steady roar of the sea, the croaking cry of a gull, the drone of some aircraft overhead. All these sounds were familiar.

I got out of the car. A gust of wind slammed the door with a sudden clap of sound. *Am I supposed to listen carefully to things like that?* I asked myself.

I climbed a dune and looked out over the deserted

beach. Here the sea bellowed so loudly that all other sounds were lost. *And yet,* I thought suddenly, *there must be sounds beneath sounds—the soft rasp of drifting sand, the tiny wind-whisperings in the dune grasses—if the listener gets close enough to hear them.*

Impulsively, I ducked down and, feeling fairly ridiculous, thrust my head into a clump of seaweed. Here I made a discovery: If you listen intently, there is a fractional moment in which everything pauses, waiting. In that instant of stillness, the racing thoughts halt. The mind rests.

I went back to the car and slid behind the wheel. Listen carefully. As I listened again to the deep growl of the sea, I found myself thinking about the white-fanged fury of its storms. Then I realized I was thinking of things bigger than myself—and there was relief in that.

Even so, the morning passed slowly. The habit of hurling myself at a problem was so strong that I felt lost without it.

By noon the wind had swept the clouds out of the sky, and the sea had a hard, polished and merry sparkle. I unfolded the second "prescription." And again I sat there, half-amused and half-exasperated. Three words this time: *Try reaching back.*

Back to what? To the past, obviously. But why, when all my worries concerned the present or the future?

I left the car and started tramping reflectively along the dunes. The doctor had sent me to the beach because it was a place of happy memories. Maybe that was what I was supposed to reach for—the wealth of happiness that lay half-forgotten behind me.

I decided to work on these vague impressions as a painter would, retouching the colors, strengthening the outlines. I would choose specific incidents and recapture as many details as possible. I would visualize people complete with dress and gestures. I would listen (carefully) for the exact sound of their voices, the echo of their laughter.

The tide was going out now, but there was still thunder in the surf. So I chose to go back twenty years to the last fishing trip I made with my younger brother. He had died during World War II, but I found that if I closed my eyes and really tried, I could see him with amazing vividness, even the humor and eagerness in his eyes.

In fact, I saw it all: the ivory scimitar of beach where we fished, the eastern sky smeared with sunrise, the great rollers creaming in, stately and slow. I felt the backwash swirl warm around my knees, saw the sudden arc of my brother's rod as he struck a fish, heard his exultant yell. Piece by piece I rebuilt it, clear and unchanged under the transparent varnish of time. Then it was gone.

I sat up slowly. *Try reaching back. Happy people are usually assured, confident people. If, then, you deliberately reached back and touched happiness, might there not be released little flashes of power, tiny sources of strength?*

This second period of the day went more quickly. As the sun began its long slant down the sky, my mind ranged eagerly through the past, reliving some episodes, uncovering others that had been completely forgotten. Across all the years, I remembered events and knew from the sudden glow of warmth that no kindness is ever wasted or completely lost.

By three o'clock the tide was out, and the sound of the waves was only a rhythmic whisper, like a giant breathing. I stayed in my sandy nest, feeling relaxed and content—and a little complacent. The doctor's prescriptions, I thought, were easy to take.

But I was not prepared for the next one. This time the three words were not a gentle suggestion. They sounded more like a command. *Reexamine your motives.*

My first reaction was purely defensive. *There's nothing*

*wrong with my motives,* I said to myself. *I want to be success-ful—who doesn't? I want to have a certain amount of recognition, but so does everybody. I want more security than I've got—and why not?*

*Maybe,* said a small voice somewhere inside my head, *those motives aren't good enough. Maybe that's the reason the wheels have stopped going around.*

I picked up a handful of sand and let it stream between my fingers. In the past, whenever my work went well, there had always been something spontaneous about it, something uncontrived, something free. Lately, it had been calculated, competent—and dead. Why? Because I had been looking past the job itself to the rewards I hoped it would bring. The work had ceased to be an end in itself; it had become a means to make money and pay bills. The sense of giving something, of helping people, of making a contribution, had been lost in a frantic clutch of security.

In a flash of certainty, I saw that if one's motives are wrong, nothing can be right. It makes no difference whether you are a mailman, a hairdresser, an insurance salesman, a stay-at-home mom or dad—whatever. As long as you feel you are serving others, you do the job well. When you are concerned only with helping yourself, you do it less well. This is a law as inexorable as gravity.

For a long time, I sat there. Far out on the sandbar I heard the murmur of the surf change to a hollow roar as the tide turned. Behind me the spears of light were almost horizontal. My time at the beach had almost run out, and I felt a grudging admiration for the doctor and the "pre-scriptions" he had so casually and cunningly devised. I saw, now, that in them was a therapeutic progression that might be valuable to anyone facing any difficulty.

*Listen carefully:* To calm a frantic mind, slow it down, shift the focus from inner problems to outer things.

*Try reaching back:* Since the human mind can hold but

one idea at a time, you blot out present worry when you touch the happiness of the past.

*Reexamine your motives:* This was the core of the "treatment." This challenge was to reappraise, to bring one's motives into alignment with one's capabilities and conscience. But the mind must be clear and receptive to do this—hence the six hours of quiet that went before.

The western sky was a blaze of crimson as I took out the last slip of paper. Six words this time. I walked slowly out on the beach. A few yards below the high-water mark, I stopped and read the words again: *Write your troubles on the sand.*

I reached down and picked up a fragment of shell. Kneeling there under the vault of the sky, I wrote several words on the sand, one above the other. Then I walked away, and I did not look back. I had written my troubles on the sand. And the tide was coming in.

*Arthur Gordon*
*Submitted by Wayne W. Hinckley*

# Octopus Odyssey

*The inhabitants of the sea have much to teach us.*
Wyland

I had a lung removed nine years ago. The doctors told me that the survival rate for the first year for my type of carcinoma was about five percent. After the initial shock subsided, I realized that I could not just sit around and wait. I had to do something. I had been a scuba diver for many years—and I wondered if that remained a possibility. Medically, I was told, there were no restrictions. Still, I was hesitant when I submerged that first time at a reef on a remote Bahamian cay. *One lung, sixty years old,* I kept thinking. Following the bubbles, I touched bottom and took short breaths. The good lung was working overtime, but it worked.

At the end of the dive, I surfaced in shallow water and switched over to snorkel. I caught an incoming current and was skimming over the sandy bottom when something in the water caught my eye. I switched direction and, to my surprise, spied a small octopus. The little creature, so far from the safety of the reef, appeared vulnerable to any predator that happened along. Intrigued, I dropped down to investigate. His large eyes immediately registered me as a threat. The small cephalo-pod brain seemed to be computing the danger in a series of signals. His soft, streamlined body convulsed in flushes of color that mutated rapidly from red to pink to green and then blue. Now he was a mottled brown that blended perfectly with the surrounding sand.

If protective camouflage wouldn't lose me, he appar-ently figured speed might work. He flew away from me in a jetlike motion, pumping water from front to back. I con-tinued to follow, hovering above him. Again he tried hid-ing, burrowing into a small clump of sea grass. Now he was virtually invisible. So far he had tried camouflage, speed and his own sort of guile, and I wondered whether he had played out his entire repertoire of evasive tactics.

Minutes later his body shuddered with color shifts. Only this time I wasn't the object of his terror. Streaking by was a school of young barracuda on the prowl for a tasty morsel like him. He quickly turned a mossy green, and the fish passed him by.

Ever so cautiously he moved off the grass and onto the sand. He was on very dangerous ground. The first to come and investigate were purple and green triggerfish. Then came a group of iridescent angelfish a foot in diameter, and finally a school of striped clownfish. They seemed to sniff and stare, but drifted away once their curiosity was satisfied. My new friend was safe once again. His color cycle was again in motion and, in a triumphant burst of scarlet that could be seen by any creature nearby, he trumpeted his return to the reef. In the blink of an eye, he dissolved into a safe network of protective corals. The drama was over. The episode took only a few minutes, but I had seen a wonderful display of fireworks and an innate desire for life.

Later on the beach, as I stripped the tank off my back and sat down, I couldn't stop thinking of that wonderful little fellow. I could see his narrow escapes, his confusion at being off the reef with barracudas searching for his flesh. His odds for survival were probably worse than mine, but he had prevailed. In a way, the encounter had brought me back to life. It's been years since my surgery, and I still go back for checkups. The doctors marvel, and I smile. How could they know about the strange and wonderful therapy that I had received on a reef on a small Bahama island?

*Mike Lipstock*

# The Sea and the Wind That Blows

I liked to sail alone. The sea was the same as a girl to me—I did not want anyone else along. Lacking instruction, I invented ways of getting things done, and I usually ended by doing them in a rather queer fashion, and so did not learn to sail properly, and still I cannot sail well, although I have been at it all my life. I was twenty before I discovered that charts existed; all my navigating up to that time was done with the wariness and the ignorance of the early explorers. I was thirty before I learned to hang a coiled halyard on its cleat as it should be done. Until then I simply coiled it down on deck and dumped the coil. I was always in trouble and always returned, seeking more trouble. Sailing became a compulsion: There lay the boat, swinging to her mooring, there blew the wind; I had no choice but to go. My earliest boats were so small that when the wind failed, or when I failed, I could switch to manual control—I could paddle or row home. But then I graduated to boats that only the wind was strong enough to move. When I first dropped off my mooring in such a boat, I was an hour getting up the nerve to cast off the pennant. Even now, with a thousand little voyages notched in my belt, I still feel a memorial chill on casting off, as the gulls jeer and the empty mainsail claps.

Of late years, I have noticed that my sailing has increasingly become a compulsive activity rather than a simple source of pleasure. There lies the boat, there blows the morning breeze—it is a point of honor, now, to go. I am like an alcoholic who cannot put his bottle out of his life. With me, I cannot *not* sail. Yet I know well enough that I have lost touch with the wind and, in fact, do not like the wind anymore. It jiggles me up, the wind does, and what I really love are windless days, when all is peace. There is a great question in my mind whether a man who is against wind should longer try to sail a boat. But this is an intellectual response—the old yearning is still in me, belonging to the past, to youth, and so I am torn between past and present, a common disease of later life.

When does a man quit the sea? How dizzy, how bumbling must he be? Does he quit while he's ahead, or wait till he makes some major mistake, like falling overboard or being flattened by an accidental jibe? This past winter I spent hours arguing the question with myself. Finally, deciding that I had come to the end of the road, I wrote a note to the boatyard, putting my boat up for sale. I said I was "coming off the water." But as I typed that sentence, I doubted that I meant a word of it.

If no buyer turns up, I know what will happen: I will instruct the yard to put her in again—"just till somebody comes along." And then there will be the old uneasiness, the old uncertainty, as the mild southeast breeze ruffles the cove, a gentle, steady, morning breeze bringing the taint of the distant wet world, the smell that takes a man back to the very beginning of time, linking him to all that has gone before. There will lie the sloop, there will blow the wind, once more I will get under way. And as I reach across to the red nun off the Torry Islands, dodging the trap buoys and toggles, the shags gathered on the ledge will note my passage. "There goes the old boy again," they will say. "One more rounding of his little Horn, one more conquest of his Roaring Forties." And with the tiller in my hand, I'll feel again the wind imparting life to a boat, will smell again the old menace, the one that imparts life to me: the cruel beauty of the salt world, the barnacle's tiny knives, the sharp spine of the urchin, the stinger of the sun jelly, the claw of the crab.

*E. B. White*
The Sea and the Wind That Blows, *1977*

# The Driftwood Queen

*My life is like a stroll upon the beach,*
*As near the ocean's edge as I can go.*

The Fisher's Boy

The ocean is, was and always will be a big part of my life. My parents were ocean aficionados, and I was introduced to its beauty and serenity at an early age. I learned to swim before I walked, had a fishing pole placed in my hands at age two and was taught how to pilot a small craft by age five—thanks to my father, who allowed me to "assist" in rowing home.

My fascination with the ocean escalated as the family spent the summer on the eastern end of Long Island on the shore of the Atlantic Ocean. I was an early riser, and by age ten I was permitted to go down to the beach in the morning to collect shells on my own. Every day I would dress quickly, grab my bucket and head for the beach. I would climb the sand dunes that hid the ocean from view and sit quietly at the top and watch the waves tumble onto the shore as I ate my breakfast roll.

One morning I noticed an older, shabbily dressed

woman walking along the beach pulling, of all things, a sled. Now and then, she would stop, pick up a piece of driftwood, examine it carefully and either discard it or place it on the sled.

I called out to her.

"Hello," I said.

She didn't acknowledge me. As only a child can, I took this as an open invitation to join the search. I looked for any driftwood that she had missed and retrieved it for her inspection. She said nothing, but seemed pleased with my company.

After a half-hour, I tapped her on the shoulder, said good-bye and started for home.

After telling my parents about my new acquaintance, my mother explained that I had met, as the town folk called her, The Driftwood Queen, or "Queenie" for short. Dad said she was a poor soul who lived in a rundown cottage near the bay. The community left food packages on her doorstep once a week, and the church collected clothing on her behalf. No one knew her real name, and many stories had circulated about where she had come from and why she collected the driftwood. Everyone had a different slant on the story, but the exact truth had never surfaced. She had become the town enigma, known only by her nickname.

My parents were kind and loving people and saw no problem with my association with Queenie. So each morning I would wait for her to appear and was always delighted at the smile on her face when she spotted me. I now carried an extra breakfast roll with me, and Queenie devoured it with gusto.

We scoured the beach, enjoying the cool ocean breeze and the feel of the ocean mist on our bodies. Although we still exchanged no words, we became friends through our daily enterprise.

One morning I saw a large piece of driftwood floating close to shore and retrieved it before it could be carried out to sea. Queenie was elated. We put the piece on her sled, which was now full, and usually that meant the end of our day together. But Queenie tugged at my sleeve and motioned for me to follow her. Before long we stood in front of a small house that had fallen into disrepair. Remembering how my father had described Queenie's home, I knew where I was.

She deposited the large piece of wood that we had found earlier next to the house, then beckoned me to follow her inside. I couldn't believe what I saw. The furniture, the cabinets, the pictures on the wall and the many exquisite-looking sculptures—all were made from driftwood.

"Queenie, did you make all these things?" I exclaimed.

She nodded her head, smiled a toothless grin and gestured for me to sit down. She left for a second. When she returned, she placed some cookies in front of me and scribbled on a large note pad. Her message said, "Hello Anne, my name is Erma. Welcome to my home."

I smiled and answered, "Hi Erma, these cookies are great, and your house is beautiful."

She reached over and patted my hands with great affection and then began to write again. "I don't talk very well, but I want you to know that I love your company."

"Me, too, Erma."

We continued our daily quests until it was time for my family to return to the city. Summer was almost over, and school beckoned. I saw tears in my friend's eyes as I said good-bye, and I assured her that I would see her next summer. She placed a small package wrapped in newspaper in my hands and kissed me on the cheek. I ran home, not turning to wave, as I knew I would cry. Inside the package was a seagull carved from driftwood. Today, some forty-eight years later, it still stands in my curio cabinet. Sadly, I never saw Erma again. My parents sat me down after school one day to say a letter had arrived from the chaplain at the hospital on Long Island. Erma had been rushed to the hospital after being found lying in the snow near her home. She had lingered for several days before she succumbed to pneumonia. Before she died, she had written a letter in front of the chaplain addressed to "My best friend, Anne."

The chaplain knew my parents and of my association with Erma and had forwarded the letter to us. It said simply: "Thank you for being my friend. I love you. Take my driftwood and make others happy. Love Erma." It took me weeks before I could talk to my parents about Erma's death. She was the first person I knew who had died. I found it hard to relate to the fact that I would never see her again. I dreamed about her, the ocean behind her smiling face, the beauty of her driftwood.

My family donated the collection to the church community center for all to see and use. I told my parents that I knew this would make Erma happy. They agreed. Every summer, the first stop we made, upon arrival, was at this small meeting hall. I would stand and gaze in awe at the items that had come from the ocean and had been transformed into works of art by my friend. Mom and Dad said they were proud of me for the kindness I had shown toward Erma. I knew I had received so much more than I had ever given. I had learned that, like the ocean, love goes on forever.

*Anne Carter*

# A Sign of Love

One morning at the Aquarium of the Pacific, three divers were preparing to feed the thousands of fish that inhabit the aquarium's 360,000-gallon Tropical Pacific Coral Reef Habitat. The first stop was the Aquarium's husbandry kitchen where the divers cut up large cubes of squid, shrimp and clams for larger fish, smaller cubes for medium-sized fish, and a blended "soup" for the very small fish. The food was then put into rubber containers that the divers could take under the water.

One of the dive volunteers would feed the smaller and medium-sized fish off to the side of the sixty-foot-wide exhibit window, and another volunteer would use his supply of food to attract the largest fish to the center of the exhibit. The feedings were always popular with visitors, so one diver had the responsibility of explaining what was going on. Bob Buck, the dive-team leader, would be the "spokes-diver." Using a special Aga-mask, Bob would answer questions from underwater via a volunteer docent stationed on the dry side of the glass.

As soon as he was in position, Bob received his first question. "Aren't you afraid of those sharks?" someone asked. Bob answered that, fortunately, the sharks in the tank had already been fed. He explained how and when sharks eat, then he took the opportunity to decry shark-finning, a practice in which fishermen remove the shark's dorsal and other fins, then dump the shark back into the ocean to die. "Can you imagine that?" Bob said. "Does this extraordinary animal deserve a death so wasteful?"

Later, a group of young schoolchildren outside the glass window caught Bob's attention. Instead of talking to each other like the other kids, these children were communicating with hand gestures. Bob, who had a hearing-impaired sister and had learned sign language, realized the children couldn't hear any of the information he'd been sharing. But he still wanted to connect with them. As a school of golden trevallies swam by, he looked at a little girl in the group and made the sign for "beautiful fish."

The children beamed!

They signed back at Bob. Their silent questions, comments and ecstatic responses filled the air. Bob continued to speak to the audience as he had done before, but now his comments were echoed by a flurry of sign language. As the presentation ended, Bob had an inspiration. He added a final thought, one that the children could take with them to always remember their first visit to this fantastic underwater world. He held out his hand and bent down two fingers. It was the sign language equivalent for "I love you!" Joy filled the faces of the children as each of them returned the love.

To this day, every diver presentation at the Aquarium includes the sign for "I love you!"

*Warren Iliff*

# Sand Castles

Hot sun. Salty air. Rhythmic waves. A little boy is on the beach. On his knees he scoops and packs the sand with plastic shovels into a bright red bucket. Then he upends the bucket on the surface and lifts it. And, to the delight of the little architect, a castle tower is created.

All afternoon he will work. Spooning out the moat. Packing the walls. Bottle tops will be sentries. Popsicle sticks will be bridges. A sand castle will be built.

Big city. Busy streets. Rumbling traffic.

A man is in his office. At his desk he shuffles papers into stacks and delegates assignments. He cradles the phone on his shoulder and punches the keyboard with his fingers. Numbers are juggled and contracts are signed, and much to the delight of the man, a profit is made.

All his life he will work. Formulating the plans. Forecasting the future. Annuities will be sentries. Capital gains will be bridges. An empire will be built.

Two builders of two castles. They have much in common. They shape granules into grandeurs. They see nothing and make something. They are diligent and determined. And for both the tide will rise and the end will come.

Yet that is where the similarities cease. For the boy sees the end, while the man ignores it. Watch the boy as the dusk approaches.

As the waves near, the wise child jumps to his feet and begins to clap. There is no sorrow. No fear. No regret. He knew this would happen. He is not surprised. And when the great breaker crashes into his castle and his masterpiece is sucked into the sea, he smiles. He smiles, picks up his tools, takes his father's hand and goes home.

The grown-up, however, is not so wise. As the wave of years collapses on his castle, he is terrified. He hovers over the sandy monument to protect it. He blocks the waves from the walls he has made. Saltwater soaked and shivering, he snarls at the incoming tide.

"It's my castle," he defies.

The ocean need not respond. Both know to whom the sand belongs. . . .

And I don't know much about sand castles. But children do. Watch them and learn. Go ahead and build, but build with a child's heart. When the sun sets and the tides take—applaud. Salute the process of life, take your father's hand and go home.

*Max Lucado*

*Guiding Light*
*Original painting by Wyland* ©2003.

# Sea of Curiosity

In my dreams, a monstrous wall of green water races my way, hissing, roaring, towering, inescapable, sweeping me into a cascading aquatic mayhem. I am lifted, tumbled, churned, pushed and fall, gasping, clawing for air. My toes touch sand; a sweet breeze soothes my lungs. I stand, choking, face the next advancing wall and leap into it, exhilarated!

In reality, when I was three the ocean along the New Jersey shore first got my attention much as it happened in the dream: A great wave knocked me off my feet, I fell in love, and ever after have been irresistibly drawn, first, to the cool, green Atlantic Ocean; later, to the Gulf of Mexico, warm and blue, serving as my backyard and playground through years of discovery; and thereafter to other oceans, to reefs, raging surf, calm embayments, steep drop-offs and the farthest reaches of the deep sea beyond. The "urge to submerge" came on early and continues, seasoned and made more alluring by thousands of underwater hours, each one heightening the excitement of the last as one dis-covery leads to another, each new scrap of information triggering awareness of dozens of new unknowns.

The lure of the sea has enticed explorers to probe the

mysteries of that vast, sparkling wilderness, probably for as long as there have been human beings. Our origins are there, reflected in the briny solution coursing through our veins and in the underlying chemistry that links us to all other life. We are probably the most versatile of creatures, anatomically gifted with an ability to climb mountains, swing among treetops, leap into the air, race across plains and briefly enter underwater realms. While we are not naturally equipped with wings to remain aloft or gills to stay submerged for long, we are endowed with ingenuity, and thus have been able to respond to another human gift, especially evident in children and those who happily never quite grow up: an irrepressible curiosity.

*Dr. Sylvia A. Earle*

# 5

# FRONTIERS OF THE SEA

*The sea never changes and its works, for all the talk of men, are wrapped in mystery.*

Joseph Conrad

# Who's Watching Who?

*Nature is the ultimate divine mystery.*

Wyland

I never considered myself the corporate type. I didn't want to sit behind a desk, and I liked to fish. So studying marine biology seemed like a natural. But after graduating college, I found myself working for the South Carolina Marine Resources Division doing exactly what I had tried to avoid: sitting at a desk crunching numbers. The job wasn't without perks, though, and occasionally I left my desk and numbers to join the research teams on multiple-day trips at sea.

The purpose of one of these cruises was to collect golden crab specimens about 120 miles offshore. Usually, we fought through rain and choppy seas. This time the sun was shining. And the glassy water made hauling in the crab traps more enjoyable, if not exactly easy. By the last day of the trip, everyone was in good spirits, satisfied that we had produced substantial data for analysis back at the lab, and we were seizing the opportunity to do some deep-sea fishing when the boat jerked into gear.

All of us looked up. Captain Pete was at the helm. He seemed to be focused on something in the distance. Keeping my hands on the rail, I worked my way toward him. "Pete," I asked. "What's going on?"

He pointed to a disturbance in the water about five hundred yards away. "There's something over there," he said. "We're going to see what it is." As the boat moved closer, I recognized the heads and flukes of whales, about twelve animals in all. The pod was mostly adults with a couple of juveniles, but the one that held our attention was the male at the lead, by far the largest of the group.

Pete slowed the boat, keeping the whales on our starboard side.

Everything about the pod seemed routine until the lead male broke away from the group, swam across the bow and turned to pass us on the port side.

I looked at Pete.

"Now what do you suppose he's doing?" I said.

Pete shrugged.

The whale passed the boat completely. He turned another 180 degrees and began to follow us. He crept closer to the stern, then moved up the starboard side into the space between the hull and the outrigger. We leaned over starboard, near the bow, as the whale swam forward beside the vessel. When he reached the water just in front of us, he rolled onto his side and looked me right in the face.

His eye was the size of a grapefruit.

I had to catch my breath. *He was checking us out!* Here was a bunch of researchers, watching the strange behavior of a whale, and we were all dumbfounded. This was a definite role reversal. The boat suddenly seemed like a big petri dish, and we were the subjects of study.

I thought about the whale the entire way home. I wondered why I always jumped at the chance to join these research teams. After all, the work was hard, the conditions were usually awful. I realized, perhaps, that it was because I instinctively needed to do it. Maybe the whale left his pod to observe us on our boat for the same reason. Maybe we're all just glorified curiosity-seekers, but it's clear there is something driving us. We often find ourselves in places we were never meant to be, seeking some little piece of the truth that we hope exists there. There are lots of researchers in the world. I was just surprised, I suppose, to discover that some of them live in the water. Now when I'm at sea, leaning over the rail of a boat, it often feels like a giant one-way mirror, and I wonder who might be observing me from below.

*Joe Moran*

# The Jonah Factor

I was new. It was the summer of 1988, and I had just started working for Howard Hall Productions, developing an undersea documentary for PBS. We were hearing reports from fishermen that a large number of "really big" whales were appearing off San Diego. The descriptions sounded like blue whales, but the odds of that were slim. But since the stories kept flooding in, we were on board, loaded and motoring toward the Los Coronados Islands in less than twenty-four hours.

I had not spent much time on the open ocean, but it was easy to tell something was different. As opposed to the usual vast expanses of empty blue water, the ocean was alive. All the animals we passed seemed to be on alert, either as predators or prey.

Large schools of anchovies at the surface were being feasted on from above by pelicans and sea gulls, and from below by Pacific mackerel. Flying fish, yellowtail jacks and the strange mola mola, or ocean sunfish, passed quickly under our boat. Blue sharks were everywhere, as they finned just below the surface. All this activity was caused by the presence of a small red shrimp, *Euphausia superba*, or krill, as it is more commonly known.

The ocean had turned blood red in huge patches one hundred feet across. The krill were being herded conveniently into tight balls by the action of thousands of small anchovies. Blue sharks materialized from all directions to gorge themselves on a free shrimp lunch. Howard and Bob Cranston had been diving with blue sharks for years and knew this type of feeding behavior had never been documented before on film. Howard was his usual calm and professional self, and Bob expertly motored our dive boat around the patches of krill. I expertly ran around the boat, yelling and pointing.

Bob shut down the boat's engines, and we drifted. We only needed to see one huge whale with a small dorsal fin and an immense blow to know we had found the blue whales we had hoped to see. The dilemma was, do you stop and film great shark behavior or try for an uncertain chance at blue whales? The unwritten rule in underwater filmmaking is, "Get it while it's hot." Wait until tomorrow, and chances are there will not be a shark or whale in sight.

I went below, loaded the camera and met Howard on the dive step of our boat, the *Betsy M.* The king of understatement said, "Try not to let any sharks bite me on the back of the head." A reasonable request, but all I could think about at the time was, *Who's going to keep the sharks from biting the back of* my *head?* Before I had time to get that question out, Howard said, "Let's go," and jumped into about three thousand feet of water in the middle of the Pacific Ocean.

It was easy to see thirty or forty blue sharks in any direction. The shark's method of feeding was to wait for the attacks of the small bait fish to herd the krill into tight balls. The sharks would approach from below, their eyes covered by a nictitating membrane, and swim through with their mouths wide open. Taking huge gulps, they seemed more like filter feeders than sharks. They ate so much their stomachs stuck out like bowling balls.

With no protection other than our cameras, my job was to keep the sharks off of Howard while he was filming. I was also told to take documentary still photographs and stay out of the way. The blue sharks immediately swam toward us to investigate, and a good bump on their nose with our fists was the only means of keeping them from swimming directly into us. The sharks seemed very fond of Howard's orange camera housing, which they bit constantly.

This was all happening within a few feet of the surface. Howard would periodically surface and look around, only to realize we were completely surrounded by whale spouts. This was just a bit more than he could take. Once the "out-of-film" signal was given, we raced back to the boat, changed film and lenses, and prepared to chase whales. Howard turned to me and very casually said, "There is no way we will be able to keep up with them in the water, so let's go wait in a ball of krill and they will come to us." As I said before, I was new. I was knee-deep in that "I'll-follow-you-anywhere" stage, so this half-brained idea seemed quite plausible at the time.

The water visibility was great, but inside the krill balls you could barely see your hand in front of your mask. So we would take turns poking our heads out to see if anyone was coming. The Jonah factor was high, and I was beginning to wonder if my day rate was a little low. All of a sudden, Howard grabbed my arm, and we swam backwards as fast as we could. A freight train, shaped like a whale, swallowed our hiding place in one gulp. We were so close it was easy to see the whale's huge eye. It looked at us both, apparently not concerned with something so small. I began to understand what one hundred feet and 150 tons really mean. I swam slowly back to the boat, wondering if I had even remembered to take a picture.

*Mark Conlin*

# Strange Discovery

Phil Dustan was a young marine biologist when the world-famous explorer, the late Jacques Cousteau, invited him on a landmark expedition to film and document the coral reefs of the Caribbean. Phil's task as "science guide" was to inspect the many reefs visited by the research vessel *Calypso* and help the ship's camera crew document coral reef ecology. During the expedition, Phil dove along the Meso American barrier reef or Belizian barrier reef with the Cousteau team, making new friends and new discoveries. But as he discovered one evening as the ship anchored at a small atoll off the coast of Belize, even the *Calypso* occasionally had its off-days.

After a delicious dinner in the *Calypso* galley, the crew prepared to film a nighttime segment on a coral reef. The stern of the ship blazed with light as a dozen divers entered the water. "The idea was to have a very dramatic show, especially our descent," Phil said. "We had four sets of lights—all connected topside by two hundred feet of cable to the *Calypso's* generators. Falco, the chief diver, led the descent, with our cameraman, Joe Thompson, filming from below and Captain Cousteau filming from behind."

Things went from bad to worse almost immediately.

First, the crew found itself surrounded by swarms of stinging jellyfish that had been attracted by the bright lights. Next, as *Calypso* held steady over the reef in about sixty feet of water, a strong wind came up and yanked the light cables away from the camera crew as *Calypso* began to swing on her anchor. The divers became "leashed fish," and the camera crew was forced to film wherever the lights went. "My job was to swim around looking scientific," Phil said, "but we kept running out of cable. Every time this happened, Falco would tap me on the fin, and we'd have to turn around and go back."

Then a great discovery was made. A crew member had located a strange new species of brain coral covered in small green spheres. The crew moved the lights in for a closer look. Phil studied the spheres carefully. Was the coral reproducing? Was it shedding eggs into the sea? Phil noticed that the eggs were wrapped in strange digestive filaments. He wracked his brain. He felt as if he had seen them somewhere before, but couldn't figure out where.

The team arranged for a scientific shot. Lights and cameras were set up, and all the divers crowded around the coral. The strange new discovery would soon be documented for the entire world to see. But something still nagged at Phil. He studied the spheres again. Where had he seen them? Finally, with the cameras running, he picked up one of the eggs and squished it between his fingers. "That's when it hit me," he said. "It wasn't a new undiscovered species. What we had 'discovered' were *petits pois* . . . the peas from dinner. The cook had thrown them overboard!"

*Steve Creech*

"It was a dark and stormy night . . ."

*Reprinted by permission of Harley Schwadron.*

# Close Encounter of the Squid Kind

While shooting the footage for *Creatures of Darkness* and *Venom!* for PBS, Howard Hall, Bob Cranston and I were working in one of our all-time favorite places, Mexico's Sea of Cortez. We were going to be filming for weeks, so our boat captain had put out the word to his friends to keep their eyes peeled for anything unusual.

One by one, local fishermen motored near our boat to tell us they were catching big squid at night. "Muy grande," they said. We had filmed squid for many years in California, so my mental picture of "big" squid ranged from six inches to about a foot. One night, we followed the fishermen to try our luck at locating the squid. The fishermen's "secret" to locating squid consisted of drifting in the middle of nowhere, over nothing in particular, in areas where the water was more than one thousand feet deep. While I loaded film in the camera, Howard and Bob lowered some bait over the side and set up the "squid" lights. These twelve-hundred-watt bulbs created a pool of light around the boat, turning night into day.

We turned on the lights and waited.

Our friend who joined us on the trip, Alex Kerstitch, was a Sea of Cortez expert. His local knowledge helped us film unusual animal behaviors we might have easily missed. Over the years, Alex had heard stories about the giant or Humboldt squid that lived in deep water. Fishermen had also told stories around the campfire, and a few specimens had actually washed up on the beach. Alex said he had dreamed of getting the chance to see a live specimen up close.

There is something about waiting—in the middle of the night—for something to swim up out of the depths that is just a little creepy. After a long time drifting, the squid started to appear below our boat, one at a time. Alex couldn't contain himself a second longer and asked if he could jump in while we were making final preparations. Howard gave him the okay, and in about a minute, Alex was gone. Five minutes later, Alex got back on the boat and went straight to bed. Howard and I were busy getting ready and really didn't think much of Alex's quick return.

The squid we saw turned out to be Humboldt squid, five feet long and weighing between seventy-five and one hundred pounds. They were just as interested in us as we were in them, and they approached us cautiously, extending one tentacle to touch us. After making contact, they would withdraw a foot or two and wait. When we reached out to touch them, the squid stayed put, changing color from white to pink to red, then back again. It was like meeting a new species on *Star Trek* for the first time!

When we looked into the dark water below, we could see hundreds of huge squid. They were in tight groups, flashing colors back and forth. The squid seemed to be frantically trying to make sense of this bright interruption in their usually dark lives.

We found out the next morning that Alex had been "mugged." Three squid had taken his collecting bags and bottles, his dive computer and the gold chain from around his neck. These squid had quarter-sized suckers, lined with teeth for tearing apart their prey, and Alex was left with a series of round, red marks circling his neck. Adding insult to injury, the squid had dragged him down very deep before letting him go.

We asked Alex if, next time, he could let us know this before we dove in.

*Mark Conlin*

"It says: All photographic-reproduction rights reserved by National Geographic Society."

# Finding His Way Home

Charles Coghlan was born in a small village on Prince Edward Island in the maritime provinces of Canada in 1841. His family came from Ireland and struggled to survive with what little they produced on the land and from the sea. When he reached the age of fourteen, friends and neighbors donated what little money they could scrape together and sent him to England for a decent education. He graduated with honors and promptly angered his mother, who wanted him to join the British foreign service, by announcing that he was going on the stage as an actor.

Shortly after, when he began to have budding success on the London stage, a gypsy fortune-teller read his future and told him that he would die at the height of his fame in a southern state of America and that his body would have no rest until he returned to the home of his birth. Coghlan related the prediction to his fellow actors, which gave them a hearty laugh, but nonetheless disturbed him for the rest of his life.

In time Coghlan became a very respected actor, touring the continent and the United States where he received standing ovations. Then in 1898, he died on stage from a heart attack while playing Hamlet in

Galveston, Texas, and was buried in the local cemetery.

Two years later, in September 1900, a horrendous hurricane struck Galveston. The sea swept over the low-lying land, carrying everything before it and killing more than five thousand people. The receding water uncovered and washed many of the coffins interred in the cemetery out to sea. Despite a sizable reward by his family and a lengthy search, Coghlan's body never washed ashore and was not found.

Eight years later, in October 1908, fishermen pulling in their net off Prince Edward Island spotted a large box floating in the water covered with sea growth and barnacles. They towed it ashore and caused a great deal of excitement in the local village, which waited in hushed anticipation to see the contents. When the slime was wiped away, it was discovered that the box was a coffin, mounting a silver plate with the body's name. They were even more astonished to find that the coffin contained the body of their famous former resident, Charles Coghlan.

The coffin was reverently carried to the little church where Coghlan had been baptized as a child, and he was finally laid to rest in the chapel cemetery.

Charles Coghlan, after eight years of drifting thousands of miles across the sea, had finally come home for good.

*Clive Cussler*

# Eyes in the Dark

[EDITORS' NOTE: *After crossing the Pacific Ocean in a light balsa raft, explorer Thor Heyerdahl recounted his adventure in his popular 1948 memoir* Kon-Tiki: Across the Pacific by Raft. *In this excerpt, Heyerdahl has a close encounter with mysterious sea creatures.*]

When night had fallen and the stars were twinkling in the dark tropical sky, the phosphorescence flashed around us in rivalry with the stars, and single glowing plankton resembled round live coals so vividly that we involuntarily drew in our bare legs when the glowing pellets were washed up round our feet at the raft's stern. When we caught them we saw that they were little brightly shining species of shrimp. On such nights we were sometimes scared when two round shining eyes suddenly rose out of the sea right alongside the raft and glared at us with an unblinking hypnotic stare. The visitors were often big squids, which came up and floated on the surface with their devilishly green eyes shining in the dark like phosphorus. But sometimes the shining eyes were those of deep-water fish that only came up at night and lay staring, fascinated by the glimmer of light before them. Several times, when the sea was calm, the black water round the raft was suddenly full of round heads two or three feet in diameter, lying motionless and staring at us with great glowing eyes. On other nights balls of light three feet and more in diameter would be visible down in the water, flashing at irregular intervals like electric lights turned on for a moment.

We gradually grew accustomed to having these subterranean or submarine creatures under the floor, but nevertheless we were just as surprised every time a new version appeared. About two o'clock on a cloudy night, when the man at the helm had difficulty in distinguishing black water from black sky, he caught sight of a faint illumination down in the water that slowly took the shape of a large animal. It was impossible to say whether it was plankton shining on its body, or whether the animal itself had a phosphorescent surface, but the glimmer down in the black water gave the ghostly creature obscure, wavering lines. Sometimes it was roundish, sometimes oval, or triangular, and suddenly it split into two parts, which swam to and fro under the raft independently of one another. Finally there were three of these large shining phantoms wandering round in slow circles under us.

These were real monsters, for the visible parts alone were some five fathoms long, and we all quickly collected on deck and followed the ghost dance. It went on for hour after hour, following the course of the raft. Mysterious and noiseless, our shining companions kept a good way beneath the surface, mostly on the starboard side where the light was, but often they were right under the raft or appeared on the port side. The glimmer of light on their backs revealed that the beasts were bigger than elephants but they were not whales, for they never came up to breathe. Were they giant ray fish which changed shape when they turned over on their sides?

They took no notice at all if we held the light right down on the surface to lure them up, so that we might see what kind of creatures they were. And, like all proper goblins and ghosts, they had sunk into the depths when the dawn began to break.

*Thor Heyerdahl*
*Excerpted from* Kon-Tiki, *1948*

# The Specialist

For me . . . a dream came true in an experience shared with my three children . . . to fly underwater in the company of a wild, free dolphin. Breaking the usual rule of "school comes first," I scooped up my small brood, ages sixteen, fourteen and eight, and enlisted their help for a week of diving and exploring reefs while working on a research project on San Salvador Island in the Bahamas. I have wistfully watched thousands of dolphins during many years spent working in, on, around and under the sea, often reveling in their exquisite mastery of ocean elements, but I had never encountered one that was willing to stay around for more than a moment in the presence of divers. I was skeptical about the existence of a wild dolphin at San Salvador who would "come right up to you." But my doubts went up in a puff of sea spray when a dark fin appeared in the distance, and a lone spotted dolphin, *Stenella longirostris*, locally known as Sandy, came straight for our boat. We stopped, looked and leaped in.

My son, Richie, making a polite overture, swam dolphinlike, undulating his whole body, holding his legs tightly together and thrusting upward with his flippers, which sent Sandy into spirals of apparent delight. The eldest, Elizabeth, blessed with a streaming mane of shining red-gold hair, was an irresistible lure. Approaching close and peppering her with rapid staccato sounds and soft, high weeps, the dolphin mouthed locks of her hair, then, eyes closed in a look of apparent bliss, gently let the strands flow through his teeth, as if trying to guess the nature of this intriguing, silky substance. Gale, an elfin eight-year-old, was the only one of us petite enough to hitch a ride. Looping her small fingers along the leading edge of Sandy's dorsal fin, she allowed herself to be towed in a circle around us, propulsion provided by thrusts of the dolphin's muscular tail. It was a living reenactment of the dolphins and cherubs depicted on ancient Roman coins and Greek mosaics.

Sandy could see clearly underwater as well as above, and so could we, using masks fitted with acrylic windows. Like all dolphins, Sandy inhaled air through a hole conveniently placed at the top of his head, and so did we, via snorkels. We also wore flippers to improve speed and maneuverability underwater. Fully outfitted with the best of modern snorkeling gear, though, we presented a pale, makeshift imitation of Sandy's exquisite design, honed during millions of years of processes that perfected slopes, angles and surfaces, coupled with finely tuned musculature, energy and sensory systems. But specialization has a price. We could comfortably enter Sandy's realm for a while, but it was hard to imagine him entering ours—to come on board and go ashore, visit a forest . . . climb a mountain . . . ride a bus. But who knows? Our great, great grandparents would have thought that flying to the moon or safely travelling to the ocean's greatest depths would be impossible for humans. Maybe someday, with the right technologies, we can invite dolphins to put on land-suits and join us for a romp on the shore.

*Dr. Sylvia A. Earle*

# Fred's Big Adventure

*There is no end to the wonders of the sea.*
Wyland

People always ask me about the big critters. What is it like to swim with dolphins? Isn't it scary to be so close to sharks? The answer I give never seems to satisfy anyone: At the end of a project, the animals I end up loving the most are usually not the big ones, but the little ones.

The creatures you really get to know are the ones you spend hours and days with. The animals that become your friends are the ones that get really tired of your noise and bubbles and lights, and allow you to become part of their daily lives.

My all-time favorite animal is an old sheep crab we found roaming among some brittle star gardens. He just seemed to be wandering slowly, pondering the complexities of crab life. The only problem was that he had a kelp forest growing on his shell.

When crabs are young, they molt their shells once a year. Molting discards a year's worth of wear and tear and anything that has become attached over that time. After getting on in years, crabs stop molting, as was the case with this particular sheep crab. He was now wearing his last shell, called a "terminal" molt. Adding to his dilemma was the small kelp plant that had started to grow on his back.

The kelp was only a minor inconvenience, since the crab walked slowly anyway, like an old man strolling through a park. The larger problem was that as the kelp continued to grow, it would begin to reach for the light of the surface. As kelp grows it produces gas bladders to keep it upright and growing toward the sun. As the plant gets bigger it creates more and more lift.

The old crab's legs were only so strong, and soon the kelp's buoyancy would overtake its ability to hold onto the bottom. Soon he would become the first-ever flying crab. His crab friends would say, "The last thing I saw was Fred being taken by the kelp aliens. It was beautiful; he just floated away."

Floating along just below the surface, Fred would be at the mercy of the meandering currents. But Fred had one last bit of luck going for him. Over time, the kelp would die and break apart in the warm surface water. No longer the rare, one-of-a-kind, balloon crab, Fred's weight would win out . . . and down he would go. As I left him, there was nothing to do but wish Fred luck—and hope he would enjoy his temporary corner of the kelp forest.

*Mark Conlin*

*Dawn of Creation*

*Dolphin Heaven*

*Mermaid and the Turtle*

*Sea of Consciousness*

*Seas of Life*

*Sea Lion Dance*

*Whale Rides*

*New Dawn*

*Moonlight Paradise*

*Original painting by Wyland* ©2003.

# 6

# SAILING
# SPIRITS

*Of Neptune's empire let us sing . . .*

*Thomas Campion*

# Last One Standing

We were long-lining for halibut out of Kodiak, Alaska, in the late winter. It was my first commercial fishing trip, and I didn't know if I could handle it. The skipper had a big debt, and he needed money. His plan was to fish the early season when the halibut were still far offshore, before the other boats got going, and maybe get a higher price for his fish. He only had one problem: His boat was too small. His was designed for inshore work in protected waters and summer weather, not a cold winter ocean fifty miles out. He had one experienced crewman, a nice kid in his twenties named Abe. Why he took a chance hiring me, a middle-aged newcomer, I'm still not sure.

As we left harbor, he spelled out what he expected of me as a green crewman. I was surprised at how easy it sounded. "Just don't lie down," he said. "Some of the toughest-looking sons-of-bitches you've ever seen can't take hard fishing. They get tired, seasick, scared, whatever. They end up laying down and quitting. You stay on your feet and keep working, and you'll be okay."

*Don't lay down? Sure,* I thought, *no problem.* The skipper showed me what to do. I had to pull an anchor out of a rack, attach a buoy, then tie on the ground-line and chuck it overboard. Then he'd drive the boat slowly away from the anchor, paying out ground-line while Abe and I attached baited hooks to it with little snaps. We laid out miles of gear this way. That's what long-lining means. It's dangerous work. You can get hooked in the clothing or the hand and get dragged off the stern by the gear. "Hooks and bait go in the water; fishermen stay in the boat." That was another one of the skipper's simple rules. We had ice on deck, a northwest wind and breaking seas. Staying on board made sense to me.

Abe and the skipper had been fishing for years and could move about casually, even with the deck rolling thirty degrees on a side and pitching out from underfoot with the occasional fore and aft wave. I couldn't. I had to hang on all the time. Just walking across the deck became a workout. My arms got tired from taking my weight, doing work my legs do ashore. I got clumsy, banging into things . . . and falling down. The skipper checked on me. I was worrying him. All he said was: "Don't fall into the ground-line reel."

I didn't fall into the big reel, but as the day and the night and the next day wore through I took some body bruises and scrapes. I mashed a hand, but didn't break it. I got weak. I tried to shake it off, to reach inside myself and gut my way through the work. But by morning my guts were in rebellion, and my strength was gone. I kept swallowing, moving around, gulping fresh air, anything to keep the seasickness down.

Sunrise was beautiful with calming seas, but for me it was too late. I had had it. After working forty-eight hours, I needed a break to heal my stomach and hug my bruises. I dragged another anchor aft, but Abe and the skipper did the job of tying on the buoy and getting the set going. I couldn't. I began snapping on hooks, carefully, trying to concentrate. But nausea took control, and I collapsed in sickness over the rail. Then again. And a third time with nothing left to toss, just ugly dry heaves as my stomach contracted. I slumped on the rail for support and stared at nothing.

I now understood what every exhausted, seasick sailor knows instinctively—that they can be healed simply by lying down. It was the one thing I'd been told not to do, and I wanted to do it badly. I wasn't thinking about my bunk either. That was much too far away. I wanted to sink straight down to the deck, seawater, fish slime, bait and all. I wanted to rest on that wet piece of steel more than I could remember wanting anything.

The ground-line kept hissing out over the stern. Abe kept snapping on hooks. I wasn't moving, and he became concerned. "Why don't you take a break?" he said. "I can finish baiting this set, and you can, uh, maybe lie down for a while?"

There it was, the one thing I wanted. But if I took a break and lay down "for a while" I wouldn't get up again until we were docked and it was time to pack my bag and go look for another job. He knew it. I knew it. I thought about it. I thought about how good just a little nap would feel. Maybe later I could get back up somehow. Maybe. Then I thought about returning to harbor with fish in the hold but no share of them mine. I thought about taking a little charity paycheck from the skipper and not meeting his eye, then walking away down the dock, with my bag in my hand and my tail between my legs.

Then I thought about it another way. I knew I couldn't stand and work. But did that mean I had to quit? Kneeling isn't lying down. Neither is crawling on your hands and knees. I wiped the goop off my chin with the back of my gloved hand, then answered Abe. "Nah," I said, "No break for me. I throw up about this time pretty much every day."

Abe laughed and shook his head. Then I laughed, too,

and the ground-line paid out without our snapping on any hooks at all until the skipper stuck his head out of the wheelhouse.

"What the hell is going on?" he yelled. "Do ya think we can catch halibut on a bare ground-line?"

I was pretty worthless for the rest of that trip. I was too sick, cold and dizzy to walk, so I actually did end up working on my hands and knees, ruining a pair of rain pants and soaking my legs in water and fish slime. I kept throwing up, too, all the way back to harbor. But for some reason the skipper didn't let me go when the trip was over. He paid me instead and kept me on for another trip and then another until I got the hang of things and turned into a real crewman. I asked him about it toward the end of the season, when I'd been with him long enough to be comfortable talking.

"Why didn't you fire me after that first trip, when I was so worthless and you and Abe had to cover my work?" I asked.

The skipper smiled. "Easy," he said. "Because you wouldn't lie down."

*Phil Lansing*

*Reprinted by permission of Harley Schwadron.*

# Geriatric Genocide

It's hot, windy and scary as we stand here on the west end of Maui, Hawaii. The eleven-mile channel between here and the island of Molokai looms as a disquieting obstacle for us and our sailboards. We can see out in the center of the channel that the heavy wind is blowing the top two or three feet right off the big Pacific swells.

Barbara Guild is a little apprehensive because she is sixty-four years old, and we're going across and back on sailboards today. Her husband, Don, is more apprehensive because he's the youngest of us at sixty-three. I'm the senior citizen of the group at sixty-five, and I'm apprehensive because the chase boat driver we hired to follow us got busted last night with the wrong stuff in his glove compartment and is sleeping it off in the slammer in Kahalui. That boat was supposed to be here in case any of us got in trouble. Now we're on our own.

The pros sailboard back and forth across this channel as though it was a small local lake. "NBD" as they call it. "No big deal." But the combined ages of the three of us total 192 years. It's different for us.

We won't drown, we know that. We've got all the right safety gear and flares and stuff. But if we don't make it across the channel and back by winter's early dark, we might have to float around all night somewhere in the chilly, rumored-to-be shark-infested ocean west of Molokai. Not a happy thought.

*Now or never*, I think, as the Walter Mitty in my soul takes over again, and we step onto our boards and sail out, leaving the warm, safe sands of Maui behind. It was Walter, of course, who brought us all here.

The first mile or two is a hoot and a half as we're all hooked in and flying. Don's flashing across the swells as he chases his wife of thirty-five years. It's like being kids again. Fifteen minutes off shore, the wind really comes up, and I take off like a cut cat dipped in turpentine.

It's a rush to fly down the face of a big swell and scare up flying fish. Most of them explode from the water and flash past my head like bazooka shells. One somehow manages to alter course at the last instant and zings between the mast and my front leg. The adrenaline rush of watching the fish is indescribable, and the distance flashes past.

In no time, it seems, there are the breakers of Molokai ahead, and I remember I have to pump the sail hard at exactly the right moment to make it through the reef. I hope I still have the reef figured out right. Automatically, my brains clicks back into 1941 mode when I first started surfing at Malibu and learned what it meant to catch a certain wave exactly right.

Success! I'm through the reef and on a glassy wave all alone. Like riding a bicycle, it all comes back.

"I made it! Yes!"

As I drag my rig up onto the tiny, eight-foot-wide beach, my friends are already scarfing down lunch and getting ready to head back. I was way behind them, and it's already four o'clock. There's no time for me to do much more than wolf down a couple of fig bars for energy and start right back.

But my sixty-five birthdays have already taken their toll on the way over, and my body feels like it's part of an eighteen-wheeler's roadkill on I-70. It creaks and groans in protest, but adrenaline helps me sail back out through the shallow reef with all of its colorful sea life flashing in the clear water below my board. The wind is light, and soon I'm out on open water and heading back.

*Piece of cake,* I think. (*Piece of cake,* I fervently hope.)

Outside the surf line, ever so slowly, as if in deference to my age and my continuing existence, the wind begins to fill, and I ease into the trapeze, then the straps. Before I know it, I am really hauling. Looking back, I can't see any other sails over my shoulder. I'm alone and flying.

In no time, I'm out into the heavier channel wind and moving so fast I'm almost hypnotized by the hundreds of flying fish I'm scaring up. Try to describe that euphoric feeling to someone, and you'll fail. Nobody else could possibly understand.

Nearing Lahaina I see a big, tourist-hauling catamaran ahead of me, roaring downwind toward home port with a boatload of sun-baked day trippers. With a little course adjustment, I could sneak up on their starboard quarter and grandstand a little. After all, I'm a senior citizen on a sailboard, just finishing a round trip to Molokai and back.

*Go for it,* my adolescent brain whispers. *Yeah . . . why not?*

I'm about a hundred yards away before any of the lobster-red tourists see me closing fast. Now it's final-decision time. Shall I really grandstand? Accelerate hard and sail right in front of the boat? Or should I take their stern now, waving as I go by, then jibe and shoot across their bow, waving again? I opt for the full showboat route.

I zip by their stern with my bald head gleaming in the afternoon sun. Senior-citizen-at-the-attack mode. But as I start to pull off a clean jibe and cut back, my tired, old body remembers that it was run over by that eighteen-wheeler today. Everything hurts, and nothing works.

I perform a rare, Olympic-style, nine-point-five catapult and plant myself facedown with a splat. Right in front of the audience.

Amidst the hoots and hollers of the Kansas catamaran crowd, I manage a water start and slink away in the direction of the Lahaina shore. Glancing back, I can now see two small yellow dots in the distance. Don and Barbara's sails. Good. I relax, knowing that my friends are not dead after all. I couldn't go back if I tried.

But will we make it in time to call off the Coast Guard? We had left instructions at a local office that if we hadn't called in, safe, by 5:30 P.M., the Coast Guard should be notified. It's already ten minutes after five, and I still have a hundred yards or so to get to the shore. Suddenly, there's no wind, so I'm swimming my rig in and it's taking forever.

Finally onshore, I start a desperate, dead-run hunt for a pay phone. Slipping and sliding, I lope through the lobby of the closest hotel, a quaint, pink, eleven-story high-rise. I find the phone after recovering my dignity from three consecutive butt slides on the ivory-slick, fake-marble floors, but the Hawaiian phone operator won't take my Colorado calling card. Swell. I'm beat, still harness-clad and disheveled from all day in the water and probably look like a homeless old bum or a mental-hospital escapee.

Swallowing what little dignity I have left, I somehow manage to panhandle a quarter from a passing senior-citizen type in a polyester dress and nurse shoes. The call gets made.

Too tired to even clean up, I remember the ten-dollar bill in my pocket and lurch to the expensive convenience store, buy a six-pack of Diet Coke and a six-pack of ice-cream sandwiches, and collapse on the beach to wait for Don and Barbara.

Ten minutes later, the three of us are sitting by our rigs, feeling the wind drop fast and watching as the sun slips into the sea. Don and Barbara look as bad as I do. And we all hurt. All over. Everything on our bodies hurts.

We can hardly talk, but Don mentions, matter-of-factly, in a quiet voice, "You know, Warren, for awhile out there today I thought we were committing geriatric genocide."

"Yeah . . . probably . . ." I say, "but where else but on the ocean could three senior citizens pull a stunt like that without getting arrested just for being too old? Not on the road. Not in the sky. Thank God there's still someplace where you never get your license lifted just for being 'over the hill.'"

*Warren Miller*

# A Shot at the Title

Ninety miles off the west coast of Sumatra, the tiny Indonesian island of Nias is heaven for professional big-wave surfers. Twenty-foot waves wrap around a submerged rocky shelf and zipper evenly closed over a distance of nearly half a kilometer. The raw power and consistency are hypnotic.

I had never surfed when I arrived on the island two weeks earlier, but I liked the title "Surfer" better than my current one, "Punk." The transition was simple. I splashed benignly about on waist-high waves falling off a surfboard I rented for a dollar. The only two "rules," as I was told by a pro from Melbourne, were, "No more than one person per wave and never turn your back on the ocean. But it's surfing, mate," he winked. "Just have fun."

And dangers? What if you hit the bottom? "Impossible," said the Melbourne pro. "It's forty feet deep out there. If you're held under, just remember: There's a flotation device—your surfboard—tied to your ankle." He referred to the leg-rope, or leash, surfers use to remain connected to their boards. "Just grab the rope," he said, "climb it to the surface . . . and you're saved! *Tidak ada masala!*" He grinned, patting me reassuringly on the back.

*Tidak ada masala* means "no problem" in Bhasa Indonesia, the national language. It's something of a countrywide motto. Everyone says it. I said it all the time myself, almost continually even. "No problem" was a good attitude, I reasoned, for the experienced, veteran traveler I was so quickly becoming. Road washed out by landslide? Well, *tidak ada masala.* Typhoid? Hey, a little typhoid never hurt anyone, *tidak ada masala.* It would still be another six weeks before a compassionate teacher in Java corrected my pronunciation. I had not, evidently, been saying "no problem" but something more closely approximating "not smelly" or "not unanimous."

The ocean reveals itself gradually. Spend half an hour just fifty feet offshore and it's clear a different paradigm exists. Terrestrial prevailing logic no longer prevails. In an ocean rain shower, "Not enough sense to come in out of the rain" is a senseless proposition. If you're in the equatorial ocean when it rains, there is zero incentive to be elsewhere. You were warm and wet; now you are warm and wet. Often in Nias it rains daily, and when it rains the ocean becomes an instrument. Drops strike still water, and the sound is bells. Syncopated, atonal—an aquatic gamelan orchestra. Surfers, we sit motionless on our boards, rain falling through us into the sea, willing conduits, lulled to trance, grateful in the serenade.

Lagundri is unique among the world's big wave surf spots. Usually, large surf carries a self-regulating feature. Paddling a surfboard out from the beach through the break or impact zone is generally only capable for those who have the skill to be out there in the first place. It's a life-saving filter on days with big waves. Weaker surfers and punks are left to flail about in the shallows.

But in Lagundri there is something called "the keyhole." The keyhole is a rocky shallow reef, which juts out perpendicular to the shore providing the point for the famous

Nias "point break." To access the surf all you have to do—
all anyone has to do—is walk out to the keyhole at the end
of the point past where the waves are breaking and hop in,
*tidak ada masalah.*

But such a hop is irreversible, resolutely irreversible—
tragically irreversible—because you then have to make
your way back to the beach the only way possible:
through the surf. The keyhole allows any punk at all to
jump in right next to the pros.

For weeks the surf has been small, playful even, and a
hop into the keyhole has resulted in no great threat. But
overnight a swell arrives. Waves explode offshore with a
force that shakes the bamboo *losmen* high on the beach.
Surfing a twenty-foot wave might be compared to jumping off a burning two-story house, landing square on your
feet, and then having the blazing house chase you down
the street.

For the experience level necessary to be in the water
today, my two weeks of small-wave frolicking leaves me,
by a conservative estimate, a decade shy. But with a mind-
less hop from the keyhole, I'm in the water.

The ocean is sentient. The messages it sends are often
whispered, indirect, carried on a current or suspended in
mist. Other times, however, the sea's communiqués are
harder to miss, even charitable. This is illustrated by my
first wave today, which neatly strips me of my shorts and
what feels like most of my body hair.

"Go home, punk," is seldom more clearly articulated.

I heed the warning, whimper audibly either "not
smelly" or "not unanimous" and paddle crazily for
shore—not merely turning my back on the ocean, but
mooning it as well. So much for the second rule of surfing.
The universe, evidently, takes a dim view of repeated
transgressions.

Victims of violent crime often cannot describe their

attackers. Similarly, I have no memory of the next wave itself, only what follows: I'm alternately dragged and bounced along the seafloor, which, thankfully, is forty feet deep and out of reach. Obediently, I pull the rope that tethers the surfboard to my leg, anticipating sweet ascension. Instead, I'm soon holding the severed and decidedly surfboard-less opposing end.

Eventually, I am washed up onto shore. Sensitive travelers careful to learn the customs of their host country please note: Few gestures are more universal than a freshly lacerated naked man trailing rope from one ankle and lavishing the beachfront with bile.

When you are violently disrobed, you may, like many, find yourself reflective. You may consider, specifically, if you still have the right to declare "not unanimous."

Merely floating on a surfboard in high seas does not make you a surfer, any more than running into a burning building with an ax makes you a fireman. To some degree, both activities are all the accreditation you need for the title "idiot." Much of the distinction of "surfer" or "fireman," for that matter, is awarded with one's ability to exit the situation gracefully. Or at least with your shorts. Fools may indeed rush in, but only surfers and firemen sashay out.

*Jim Kravets*

# Father Time

My father gave me a lot of things: my awkward gait, exceptional eyebrow coordination, a balding head (maternal grandfather, yeah right). He gave me his love for arguing and sense of righteous indignation. And while Dad wasn't a believer in handing his kids their every wish, he also gave me my first surfboard.

It was the summer of 1981. My brother and I were spending our annual court-appointed and parent-approved two months in Texas. Most of these days consisted of hanging at my dad's on Galveston Bay—nowhere near the island surf spots—the flattest portion of a notoriously flat body of water, with none of the excitement of our beach life back home. Pops must have predicted our postpartum depression, because when we arrived he unveiled a pair of new toys for my brother and I. They weren't the best-made boards, but we thought they were perfect. And late that summer we spent a week in Florida, where I discovered the full realm of first-time surfing experiences—and where, just a few years later, my father would embark on a life-changing mission of his own.

My dad never joined in on that first surf trip. And I doubt we even stepped out of our narcissistic playground to invite him. But I know he tried surfing at least once before I was born when my parents lived in Del Mar. He had borrowed my uncle's '68 "Hawaiian V," caught a couple waves, and on the way back out stepped on a stingray, which pierced his ankle straight through. As boys, my brother and I would constantly ask him to repeat the story and marvel over the scar and how bad it must have hurt.

Of course, Dad didn't find the story nearly as entertaining. And I'm sure his pride hurt more than his ankle. Pops wasn't used to setbacks. From his youth he excelled at everything, from grades to football, ending up at the Naval Academy where he became an aviator, eventually flying jet aircraft and, ultimately, the space shuttle.

By the time Dad's first mission came along in 1984, I'd been surfing for a few years. In fact, I'd already replaced the board he'd given me with one I proudly paid for myself. And while the focus of our family's Florida adventure was my father's maiden voyage into space, it was also my first surf trip. And with two weeks of waiting between launch and landing, I was frothing at the thought of surfing what were surely some of the best waves in the world. My mom had barely put the car in park before I hit the water, and when the waves died I toured around the various Cocoa Beach institutions to continue my surfing education on land.

I paced the maze at Ron Jon's almost daily, getting a permanent crick in my neck from checking out the hundreds of boards hanging on the ceiling and keeping an eye out for hot pros like Matt "Kech Air" Kechele. I catalogued all this information for a later date, intent on wowing my friends with these strange, wonderful discoveries upon my return. Meanwhile, my dad floated weightless above the Earth, concentrating on launching and retrieving satellites, never considering the chain of events he'd set in motion miles below.

Over the next ten years, I surfed each return trip to Cape Canaveral to watch my dad catapult into the unknown. And during his final mission in 1995, I even crammed my board onto a visitors' bus so I could surf in front of the astronauts' beach house. Dad, of course, was unable to participate for fear of endangering the mission. But when he retired the following year and took a job closer to Earth in San Diego, he immediately expressed interest in learning to surf. And I was eager to comply. I arranged to have a longboard shipped to his house and gave him the inside tip on what kind of wetsuit to buy. Then I waited patiently for his first post-surf report.

"Well, son," he told me, "I've just been so busy. I barely get time in an airplane anymore. But next time you visit, we'll go."

When my winter vacation finally clocked around, I dutifully scheduled two weeks in San Diego. And when the pilot reported it was raining in Southern California and would be for another week, I never even unpacked my board bag. Two days later I was in sunny Hawaii.

Dad didn't blame me a bit. He may not have surfed, but he understood what it was like to have an all-consuming passion. And he had sacrificed plenty to push his personal flying limits. Nonetheless, when he moved back to Texas the following year and sold the surf gear, I couldn't help but hear the closing chorus of "Cat's in the Cradle."

But I still had hope of sharing that indescribable feeling with the man who'd given me the tools to start. Until, one spring, I finally figured it out.

I was camped out on a secluded point break in central Baja. We'd driven for two days down dirt roads and across salt flats just to futz around in tiny surf for three days and babble beneath the stars at night. It was a blast. My dad was much on my mind these days, and at one point I watched a slow crumbler roll through and thought, *This is it.* I'd get Dad in a car with a couple of boards. We'd hit the road south and spend a week charging around Mexico. Speak some Spanish, drink some beers, argue life's more trifling matters. Maybe we'd even get lucky and get in the water. I was still contemplating the details as we packed the trucks the next morning and giddily blazed off to Cabo to see if we could find something legitimate to ride.

Less than two days later I fled Baja's tip and was standing at my father's side in a Houston hospital as he grappled with the cancer that he'd only been diagnosed with a month earlier. It seems things weren't nearly as positive as the early tests predicted. In three days he would pass away. We spent the bulk of that time around his bed, holding tight to every moment and memory, saying our final sentiments while simultaneously trying to maintain the illusion that none of it was really happening.

He'd given it all to me: the first equipment, the support to stay in the water and the encouragement to write about it. And in twenty years, not once did he say, "Why haven't you taken me surfing?" Instead he apologized for me having to cut my Baja trip short "just to come see him."

But that's being a father. Dad got more joy by watching me embrace something unspeakably special than he could have ever experienced by keeping it to himself. And I suppose that's the essence of a true gift.

*Matt Walker*

# Surfer

[EDITORS' NOTE: *In his 1872 memoir* Roughing It, *the ever-adventurous American storyteller Mark Twain recounts the strange Hawaiian custom of riding waves on a thin board.*]

The surfer would paddle three or four hundred yards out to sea, taking a short board with him, then face the shore and wait for a particularly prodigious billow to come along; at the right moment he would fling his board upon its foamy crest and himself upon the board, and here he would come whizzing by like a bombshell! It did not seem that a lightning express train could shoot along at a more hair-lifting speed. I tried surf-bathing once, subsequently, but made a failure of it. I got the board placed right, and at the right moment, too; but missed the connection myself. The board struck the shore in three quarters of a second, without any cargo, and I struck the sand about the same time, with a couple of gallons of water in me.

*Mark Twain*

# Two Battleships

[EDITORS' NOTE: *The story of "Two Battleships" was widely circulated during World War II. As a "Tin Can" sailor in the United States Navy, Maurice Ricketts spent six years on destroyers in the North Atlantic and South Pacific. According to Ricketts, who heard this story more than sixty years ago, such incidents didn't always make it into the ship's official log.*]

An aircraft carrier had been at sea in heavy weather for several days. As night fell, a patchy fog rolled in, so the captain remained on the bridge to keep an eye on all activities. Shortly after dark, the lookout on the wing of the bridge reported, "Bright light ahead, sir."

"Is it steady or moving astern?" the captain called out.

The lookout replied, "Steady, captain." That meant the ships were on a dangerous collision course.

The captain called out, "Signal that ship: 'Please divert your course fifteen degrees to the north to avoid collision.'"

Back came a signal, "Recommend you divert YOUR course fifteen degrees to the south."

The captain said, "Send: 'This is the captain of a United States Navy ship. I say again, divert YOUR course.'"

"I'm a seaman second class," came the reply. "YOU had better change YOUR course."

By that time the captain was furious. He spat out, "Send, 'THIS IS THE AIRCRAFT CARRIER *ENTERPRISE*, WE ARE A LARGE WARSHIP. DIVERT YOUR COURSE NOW!'"

Back came the signalman's light, "This is a lighthouse on a land mass straight ahead."

*Maurice Ricketts*

# The Bond Between a Captain and His Ship

*CAPT: I am the Captain of the Pinafore.*
*ALL: And a right good captain, too!*
*CAPT: I'm very, very good, And be it understood,*
*I command a right good crew.*

From *H.M.S. Pinafore*

Captain Elijah G. Baufman was a big, jovial man, his leathery skin tanned by many years of sun, wind and storm. He was an expert mariner and a friend to all who knew him. He loved the sea and the poems of Robert W. Service.

For his ship, the S.S. *Humboldt,* the captain had a special and very deep love. She was his "little girl," a member of his family. He kept the small, trim and sturdy steamer spotless and gleaming.

Built in 1897, the *Humboldt* began her career during the '98 gold rush to Alaska as a passenger and freight carrier out of Seattle. It is estimated that she brought gold valued at $100 million safely out of Alaska and went to the rescue of more than a thousand shipwrecked persons.

Captain Baufman was the only master she ever knew. For thirty-seven years he guided her through storm and sunshine, blizzards and fog. His affection for her, his pride in her accomplishments, were frequent topics of conversation along the Pacific Northwest waterfronts. He turned down offers to skipper large ocean liners to remain with his little ship.

But time is as relentless as the tides, and in 1934 both the captain and his ship were heavy with years. Newer, faster vessels had succeeded the *Humboldt*. And the time had come for Captain Baufman to retire.

The captain seldom cried, but tears ran down his weather-worn cheeks when the *Humboldt* was taken south from Seattle to San Pedro, California. There she was placed with other old, forlorn vessels in the ship graveyard, eventually destined to be reduced to scrap. Captain Baufman, with his memories and still pining for the sea, moved to San Francisco.

Less than a year later, on August 8, 1935, just at "sunset and evening star," Captain Baufman closed his eyes for the last time and "crossed the bar."

That same night, four hundred miles south, the Coast Guard cutter *Tamaroa* was near the San Pedro harbor when the crew noticed an old steamer, outward bound, holding a true course for the channel. No smoke came from her funnel. Dark and silent, with only one red warning light glowing at her stern, she was headed for the open sea.

It was the *Humboldt*.

When no answer came to the guardsmen's challenge, the cutter swung ahead of the ship and launched a boat. But the boarding party found the ship deserted, the wheel in the pilothouse unmanned.

Whatever force it was that slipped the moorings loose from the *Humboldt* and guided her through the harbor, it was not strong enough to resist the towlines of the cutter. The ship was returned to the graveyard and her final destiny.

*Vincent Gaddis*

# Sailsmanship!

John Cacciutti dove into the water to snare his prize catch—after it had swiped his rod and reel!

During a vacation in Acapulco, Mexico, in 1989, Cacciutti, of Wallingford, Pennsylvania, his wife, Terry, and four friends chartered a boat and went looking for sailfish. Within a couple of hours, Terry and a friend had each caught two sails. Everyone was having a good time as Cacciutti settled into a chair on the bridge of the boat, sipping a cool drink.

Suddenly, like the crack of a whip, the rod in the bridge rod-holder snapped from the outrigger and started dumping line at an alarming rate. Cacciutti quickly pointed the rod at the fish, locked up the drag and set the hook hard. "Up out of the water came a beautiful nine-foot Pacific sailfish," he recalled. "The bridge was a great vantage point to watch this aerial action, but it was no place to fight a fish. I needed to get back down on deck."

Cacciutti took the rod and reel and started down the ladder when he slipped and fell onto the deck below.

"Unfortunately, the rod and reel didn't make this journey with me," he recalled. "As I was falling, I tried to pull a six-foot rod sideways through a three-foot ladder hole, but the rod had its own idea and shot from the bridge like an arrow. We all watched in amazement as the rod sailed high over our heads and splashed into the water."

Then they saw the sailfish make a few jumps before sounding into one thousand feet of water. While Cacciutti sulked and tried to shake off his embarrassment, one of his friends on the bow spotted the sailfish still dragging the rod and reel. The boat pursued the fish and came close to it several times, but each time the sailfish sounded again.

"All the hopes and dreams I had of recapturing that fish quickly faded," Cacciutti said. "I went to the bow and stared into the deep blue water as thoughts of defeat raced through my mind. Suddenly, I spotted the fish again next to the boat. I knew there was no more time for thought or words to the crew.

"I dove off the starboard bow with my hands outstretched and hit the water behind the big fish. I swam about twenty feet down and grabbed onto the taut fishing line. With my lungs about to burst, I made it to the surface for a breath of air.

"Meanwhile, the big fish was running away from me, and the line was burning my hand. But then the line slowly became slack, and I began to worry about the fish and its sixteen-inch bill. Could it be charging me this very second? My heart was pumping from fear as I swam toward the boat. But fortunately the sail didn't charge, and I climbed back onto the deck."

Once on board, Cacciutti continued to pull in the line hand over hand until, up from the depths, sprang the rod and reel. The soaking-wet angler grabbed hold of the rod with two hands, quickly took in the slack, and pulled and cranked in one thousand feet of line. Finally, he reeled in the tired fish until it was alongside the boat. With heavy gloves on his hands, the first mate then leaned over the side and grabbed hold of the bill of the sailfish.

"I got a baseball bat and was ready to subdue the fish when the captain and his mate shouted for me to release it," said Cacciutti. "After thinking about it, I decided that the greatest trophy would be in the pictures that my wife was taking and the story about this catch. There was no need to kill this great fish."

After measuring the sail, they pulled it along in the water, forcing water through its gills, which helped to revive it. "The fish began to move his big tail, so we gave him a push and set him free," said Cacciutti. "The sailfish returned to the sea to fight again."

*Bruce Nash and Allan Zullo*

Raymond the lunatic and his far-fetched
tale of alien abduction.

# First Homecoming

My husband, Alan, and I had just had our first baby when we purchased our first commercial fishing boat. Our "new" boat, the *Valiant,* was a thirty-six-foot salmon seiner, fifteen years old and in sound, if worn, condition. Its problems included a tired engine, leaky hydraulics and extremely sloppy steering. It was impossible to drive the boat in a straight line. It seemed to always move at an angle. But it was June and the fishing season was upon us, our only chance to make all the money we'd need for the year. We'd have to live with our zigzagging boat and fix things over the winter. For the moment we were proud new owners taking our place in the fleet after years of crewing for others.

The mainstay of our income was salmon, but twice a year we were given twenty-four-hour periods to fish for halibut. The huge bottom fish had become abundant in the waters off Kodiak and fetched a good price. Fishing for halibut meant switching to hook-and-line gear and traveling far offshore. It was a race to fill the boat in twenty-four hours. That alone made it dangerous, but bad weather on the designated day could be especially perilous. With some nerve and a little luck, fishermen could make a great deal of money in a very short time, and the temptation ran high to ignore storm warnings and risk everything.

I'd baked a huge lasagna and brownies for Alan and his crew. There was no time for cooking or sleeping on these twenty-four-hour openings. Every moment would be spent either setting or hauling gear. I walked down the wooden ramp to the dock, baby in a backpack and food in arms. The harbor was full and every boat lively with last-minute chores. Decks were piled with gear, and crewmen called to each other as they cut bait, sharpened hooks and coiled ground-line. At our boat, Alan's two young crewmen sat surrounded by tubs of salted herring, cheerfully bopping to their music as they baited two thousand shiny new hooks. If things went well on this trip, we stood to make a lot of money, of which they'd earn a hefty crewshare. It was hard not to tally the imaginary pounds of fish in my head. If Alan filled the boat, we could make as much as fifty thousand dollars. Even after expenses, that would be enough to make the boat payment and pay off the hospital bills for the baby's somewhat difficult birth. I was excited and nervous, especially about the weather.

As I stepped on the boat I saw Alan through the window, his head bent over a chart. He looked worried. The National Weather Service marine forecast scratched over the VHF radio, a flat voice repeating the local conditions: Area 3A, winds Easterly at fifteen knots, increasing to thirty-five by Tuesday night. Not good.

When Alan saw us his face transformed. His furrowed brow and intense concentration melted into an open and affectionate smile. He always had a wonderful smile for me, but it was even more wonderful for the baby. I loved the unaffected joy that flowed from him in her presence.

"Well, I guess we're ready," he said.

"Knock 'em dead, honey," I said, then more softly, ". . . and be careful."

Two nights later I lay in bed at home listening to the wind howl at the predicted thirty-five knots. Our cabin was nestled in tall spruces a half-mile from the sea, but I could still hear the buoys moaning off the point. I wondered where Alan had chosen to go. Knowing him, he'd find his own patch of ocean to fish and wouldn't follow anyone's advice. The baby cried out in her sleep, and I murmured not to worry. I thought about all the boats scattered off the coast at this moment, working through the night in the waves and wind. All out in the same ocean, yet each one alone and vulnerable to an indifferent sea. I fell asleep praying for all of them to come home safely.

The next evening I walked to the high bridge that spanned the channel entrance to town to watch for returning boats, but only a few came back. The *Valiant* wasn't among them. I went home and waited another night. The storm was still with us, and I comforted myself with the knowledge that they weren't out fishing in it. They were most likely anchored, safely waiting out the weather.

In the morning I went looking again. Boats offloading fish lined the cannery docks, and the harbor was nearly full. But still no *Valiant.* I went to the cannery where we sold our fish and saw one of Alan's buddies in the middle of unloading. Bags full of huge fish were being lifted out of his hold with a crane. I called down to him, had he seen Alan?

"Saw him the morning before it opened, up by Black Cape, but I don't know where he ended up. He's not back yet?"

I shook my head, no.

"Oh, you know Alan. Don't worry. He'll turn up."

But he didn't turn up all that day, and I was beginning to worry. I spent a sleepless night waiting for the phone to ring and imagining my own call to the Coast Guard. When the baby woke in the morning, I headed back to the bridge. The sun flared over the edge of the sea. A light fog wisped between the islands to the east and turned golden as sunlight spread horizontal across the sea. I was filled with sudden hope that Alan would be safely in the harbor, that my nightmare would be over instead of just beginning. But when I got there I saw that the slip was empty. The last empty slip in the harbor.

I walked back to the bridge and breathed in the cool sharp air carried in on the tide. It smelled of salt and kelp and an ocean full of life. The baby must have smelled it, too, and laughed, squirming in the pack. On the horizon was a boat, too far away to identify. I watched it until I noticed how it zigged and zagged its way slowly up the bay and toward the channel. There was only one boat like that in the fleet, and my heart was on it.

I could see that the *Valiant's* waterline was as high as when she'd left port, and I knew what that meant. There was no load of halibut from this trip. No fifty thousand or thirty or even five thousand dollars. While I was disappointed, I could only imagine what Alan and his crew had been through during the last three days. Three days of fighting wind and tide, equipment failure and God knows what other disasters.

I waited until the *Valiant* was tied up before approaching the slip. I stepped quietly onto the deck as Alan emerged from the engine room, and we stood much as we had three days, a lifetime, before. He looked exhausted, shellshocked, his face streaked with grease. He wiped his hands with a rag and managed a small smile. "Bad weather out there," he said, unable to hide his disappointment. He'd wanted this load as bad as anyone. "We tried everything we could, but . . ."

"It's okay," I said. "It doesn't matter."

He didn't answer. There was nothing else to say. He'd made it through his three days of hell, and I'd made it through my own. The harbor was calm, and the boat was still floating. The baby reached out, laughing, for her father. "Are you ready to go home?" I asked.

"More than you can imagine."

*Leslie Smith*

*Sea Turtle Reef*

*Original painting by Wyland* ©2003.

# $\overline{7}$

# ON COURAGE AND ADVENTURE

*A* life on the ocean wave!
A home on the rolling deep,
Where the scattered waters rave,
And the winds their revels keep!

*Epes Sargent*
Life on the Ocean Wave

# Lost in the Atlantic

"Matthew, see how the water is lighter around the island, where it's shallow?" Mike Sperber said to his fourteen-year-old son. "In a while the bottom will drop off, and you'll see a color change."

Matthew obediently pressed his face against the window of the twin-engine Aero Commander 500 and watched the Atlantic Ocean below change abruptly from light blue to almost black. He'd enjoyed fishing in the Bahamas with his dad and his dad's friend, J. B. Stephens, but he sometimes wished his dad wouldn't push so hard. Everything was "see this" or "do that." Still, he wasn't ready to go home to Florida yet.

"That's where the really big fish are," Sperber continued, pointing down. "Tuna, marlin—even sharks." Seated next to pilot Jerry Langford, Sperber glanced back at his son. It was 5:20 P.M. on Sunday, August 4, 1991.

Suddenly, a loud bang made them jump. "Dad?" Matthew said. "What's—"

A second loud bang drowned out his voice. The plane's engines fell silent. Matthew gripped the sides of his seat as the plane shuddered, then started dropping.

Langford desperately turned to the radio's emergency

frequency. "Mayday! Mayday!" he shouted. "We're going down!"

The stunned passengers strapped on life jackets. "Matthew!" his father said. "When we hit the water, don't wait for me. Get out fast. Understand?"

"Yes, sir." Matthew's heart pounded, making it hard to breathe. His seat was dropping out from under him like a runaway roller coaster. Seconds before the plane hit the water, he screamed, "Dad, I love you!"

At home in West Palm Beach, Florida, Betty Sperber was baking a chocolate cake. The dark-haired nurse expected Mike and Matthew for dinner around five-thirty.

Six o'clock came and went. Just before seven P.M., a friend of J. B. Stephens called with the news: "Their plane went down in the ocean!"

Betty listened in disbelief. When she hung up, nightmarish images rose before her eyes. She moaned and covered her face. "Don't let them be dead," she sobbed.

The plane hit the water with an explosive roar, smacking across the surface like a skipping rock. Matthew was tossed forward as the fuselage ripped apart and water rushed in.

"Get the door open!" Sperber yelled to Stephens, who was closest to the exit. Stephens, a big, bearlike man, began shoving outward with all his strength.

"It's jammed, Mike!" he yelled. Sperber struggled back through the rising water to help. Matthew reached down to unfasten his seat belt. To his horror, it, too, was jammed. "Dad!" he screamed. "I can't get my seat belt off."

As Stephens continued to ram his massive shoulder against the now-submerged door, Sperber turned to help Matthew. The pilot was out of his seat, his life jacket hanging loosely around his neck. He was holding the back of his head. Only a small pocket of air remained near the cabin's ceiling. If they didn't find a way out within seconds, they were all going down with the plane.

Water was lapping over Matthew's chin when his father's desperate effort to free him finally worked. At the same moment, Stephens punched the door out against the pressing sea, then reached back to grab his friend's son. Without hesitating, he dived out, dragging the teenager along.

The swim to the surface seemed to take forever. When Matthew finally burst through the water, he drew a deep, gasping breath. Air!

Stephens pulled Matthew to the plane's wing. "Hang on!" he said, and started back to help the others. Seconds later, Sperber popped up in the water and joined his son by the wing. Finally, the pilot surfaced. He looked dazed, and his life jacket was gone. Stephens grabbed his arm and helped him over to the others.

The plane was slipping below the water. "We need to get away from here!" Sperber said. They dog-paddled furiously, taking turns helping the injured pilot.

About twenty feet away, the four looked back. The plane was hovering just beneath the surface. After a long moment's hesitation, it tilted down and slid through the crystal-clear water into the black depths.

Soon Sperber took charge. "Let's hook our life jackets together," he suggested. "The current here is strong. We don't want to get separated."

Stephens was still supporting the injured pilot in his arms. "Jerry here is bleeding pretty bad," he said. "He's going to need some help to stay afloat."

Matthew looked over at the pilot, noticing that his hair was matted with blood. His father glanced over, too, then asked Stephens quietly, "What about the graycoats?"

Matthew frowned, puzzled. What was he talking about? Then, with a chill, he understood. Sharks! Sharks could sense blood in the water.

"Uh, Mike," Stephens said, "I think we'd best not talk about that. What can we do about Jerry?"

After trying several arrangements, they used Langford's pants to make a kind of hammock, tying the legs to Matthew's and Stephens's life jackets. The pilot lay between them, resting his head on Mike Sperber's jacket.

The sun edged lower in the sky, sending brilliant orange and red reflections across the water. The four drifted in silence, pushed along by the Gulf Stream. Finally, Matthew heard a faint, rhythmic *thup-thup-thup*. "What's that sound?"

The others heard nothing. "Look!" Matthew said excitedly, pointing south. "A helicopter!"

Flying at low speed, the helicopter made a beeline for them. They yelled and waved, then watched in stunned disbelief as it kept going. "Why didn't they see us?" Matthew demanded. "They were right on top of us!"

"From the air, we're just little specks," Sperber said slowly.

The night passed slowly. Searchlights from aircraft and boats crisscrossed the dark water to the south and east, but none came close.

Matthew was growing sleepy when his father said quietly, "Try to stay awake, Matthew. Your eyes and ears are sharper than ours. We need you."

Matthew was surprised, but pleased. "Okay, Dad. I'll do it." The water grew cool, then cold. Matthew shivered, fighting to keep his eyes open. It took an effort not to think about the huge predators that moved through those dark waters.

Dawn brought warmth and light. But as the morning wore on, they all began to blister in the sweltering sun. To shield themselves from the sun, they ripped off their T-shirt pockets and plastered them across their foreheads.

Matthew licked his dry lips. He was thirsty and hungry.

His life jacket had rubbed the skin on his neck till it was raw.

It was nearly noon when he heard something again. "Dad! A plane!" They soon spotted it—a Coast Guard jet. As it got closer, they splashed and waved.

The jet was about a mile away when it abruptly banked to the west. Sperber lowered his arms. "It didn't see us," he said flatly. "It's just flying a grid pattern."

Matthew's heart sank. Then his father shouted, "Look! A boat!"

A huge sport-fishing boat was cruising toward them, sending a faint sound of music across the water. Soon it was close enough for them to see a man and woman relaxing in lounge chairs, drinks in hand.

"Over here!" Stephens bellowed.

Matthew put his fingers in his mouth and let loose an ear-splitting whistle. *If they didn't hear that,* he thought, *they're deaf!*

The boat, now just one hundred yards away, showed no signs of slowing down. "Stop!" the four screamed. "Help us!" The couple never looked up as the boat cruised away.

They fell silent after that, too miserable even to talk. No other planes or boats came near. As the sun dipped below the horizon and the ocean cooled, they all started shivering uncontrollably. The night before, they had still had energy to fight the cold; now they were weak and dehydrated. How could they stand another night in the dark water?

Matthew was drifting along, only half-awake, when something hit his left arm like a hot razor blade. He screamed as slick, stringy tentacles drifted across his arm—a Portuguese man-of-war! The purplish, balloonlike creature floated along, trailing poisonous tentacles to sting and paralyze its prey. Matthew sobbed with fear and pain as his father and the other men pulled him away.

"Dad," he cried hysterically, "I'm cold. I'm tired. I want to go home. I don't want to die!"

Sperber pulled him close. "None of us is going to die. *They're going to find us.* You hear me?"

Matthew looked up. In the moonlight, his father's face was tinged with blue. "Matthew, I . . ." Sperber's voice faltered. "I never really tell you, but I hope you know I love you."

Matthew drew a shaky breath. "I know," he said, calmer now. No matter what happened, at least they'd be together.

Over the next few hours, they drifted in and out of a miserable half-dozing state, too cold to sleep and too exhausted to stay awake. Langford, the weakest of the four, wasn't going to last much longer.

Early Tuesday morning, the sun peeped weakly from behind dark storm clouds. Soon the wind picked up, and the sky darkened. Whitecaps began to form, leaving them bobbing in increasingly rough seas. Matthew got a better grip on the injured pilot.

Langford turned his blistered face toward the others. "Maybe we ought to pray," he said hoarsely. As the storm swept upon them, the frail pilot offered a simple prayer for their rescue.

Betty Sperber woke Tuesday morning, feeling a restless urge to get out of the house. She dressed quickly and called a neighbor. "I want to go to church," she blurted out.

A few minutes later they pulled up to the church, and Betty quickly found the pastor. "I've been praying at home," she said, "but I just feel it isn't good enough."

The minister took her hand and bowed his head. "Lord, you see the tiniest sparrow that falls from the sky," he prayed. "I ask that your eyes will be on Mrs. Sperber's loved ones, wherever they are."

The storm burst in all its fury upon the four in the water. As heavy raindrops pelted them and cold waves tossed them up and down, they clung together. Desperate for a drink, they tried to catch rain in their mouths.

At last the storm swept past, and the sun appeared. Suddenly, Matthew's head jerked up. "I hear a plane," he announced. Search planes were returning to the area.

They tensed. This might be their last chance. Sperber collected watches and other metal objects, hoping they might be picked up by radar.

The jet was almost upon them. Sperber held the metal bunched in one hand and used his other hand to tilt his credit card, hoping the shiny hologram might reflect the sun. Yelling, Stephens also flashed his credit card. Langford used both hands to wave. Matthew thrashed the water with his life jacket. *Maybe,* he thought, *the white foam would catch the pilot's eye.*

Seconds later the jet screamed above them and disappeared. Two minutes passed, then three. Nothing.

"It's coming back!" Matthew yelled. "Everybody splash!"

Once again, he thrashed the water into a white foam. The others joined in. When the jet got closer, Sperber cried out triumphantly, "They see us!"

The four erupted in cheers as the jet dropped a canister that hit the waves and sent a streamer of smoke into the sky. Soon a helicopter raced toward them. It landed on the surface about fifty feet away. A crew member held a chalkboard with the words, "ONE AT A TIME!"

Slowly, they swam toward the helicopter, the two men helping the injured Langford along. After two long days, it was over.

The sun-blistered survivors were taken to St. Mary's Hospital in West Palm Beach. Betty Sperber greeted her husband and son with a joyful cry. "Thank God you're alive!" she sobbed. "I've been praying . . ."

Mike Sperber smiled. "We did some praying out there, too," he admitted. "And this kid—he really handled himself out there." He looked at Matthew. "I'm proud of you, son."

*Deborah Morris*
*Adapted from* Real Kids Real Adventures *series*

# One Hundred and One Atlantic Nights

*Courage is like love; it must have hope to nourish it.*

Napoleon Bonaparte

I arrived home to a message light flashing on the answering machine. Nothing really out of the ordinary, and yet I had an uneasy sense about it. I pushed the button and listened to the devastated voice of my twenty-one-year-old son, Daniel:

"I'm guttered, Mum. Jaish can't do it!"

I gasped, feeling his disappointment and my own as well. Three months before, in the fall of 1995, Daniel's old school chum Jaishan had asked Danny to team up with him and enter the Great Atlantic Rowing Race and row from Tenerife, Canary Islands, to Port St. Charles, Barbados. He had accepted with great excitement. They paid the entrance fee, and planning began immediately.

I was excited to be able to use my background in public relations to help promote them, get the specially designed rowing boat custom built and raise the needed funds. We had two years.

Both boys were British army cadets and needed permission for the time off. Danny's request had been accepted. Now we knew Jaish's request had been turned down. I reassured Daniel that he would easily find another partner.

"It's not that easy, Mum. I need someone who can commit the next two years to promotion, fund-raising, training and skills acquisition. But mostly it has to be someone I can spend three months alone with on a twenty-three-foot boat!"

I'm not really sure what happened next. I don't know whether he asked or I offered. All I know is that at the end of the conversation, I had agreed to become his new partner and row across the Atlantic with him—we were a team!

My beloved second husband, Keith, had died of cancer a few years before, and my old life was gone. I was fifty years old and a widow. My life felt empty and had no direction. The prospect of spending the next two years preparing for an adventure was very exciting, and the opportunity to share this unique experience with my son was irresistible. Once I had decided, there was no going back. He was offering me a once-in-a-lifetime opportunity, and I was going to seize it.

The commitment to row the Atlantic had been made. Now came the logistics. Money was a major issue. I had a marketing job, but there was no way it would begin to finance this project. So off I went to the bank.

As the former mayor of my hometown of Chipping Norton, I was fairly well known, so I did have some hopes. But when all was said and done, my presentation still sounded like a fifty-year-old widowed woman asking for a loan so she could row the Atlantic with her son. Right!

So I mortgaged my home, my two-hundred-year-old little stone cottage.

We were officially a team.

When our custom-built, ocean-going rowing boat was completed, we ceremoniously named it *Carpe Diem*—Seize the Day! We began training sessions, mostly on the Thames. Daniel began to feel quite guilty because of the financial burden he felt he had placed on me. At one point I realized, *My God, if this doesn't work, I could lose my house!* But we didn't have time for thoughts like those. We each brought our own unique skills to the venture. I knew it was my job to get us to the starting line in the Canary Islands, and Captain Daniel would get us to the finish line in Barbados.

When I finally got up the courage to tell my own mum of our plans, to my delight she offered no guilt, fear or negativity. Instead her response was: "The years between fifty and sixty go like that!" and she snapped her fingers. "DO IT! And I'm utterly behind you."

October 12, 1997, finally arrived. After two years of hard work, we departed Los Gigantes Tenerife along with twenty-nine other teams. At fifty-three, I was the oldest participant, and we were the only mother-and-son team. Our boat was designed with two rowing seats, one behind the other. For the first six hours we rowed together. After that, we began the routine we would maintain for the next one hundred days. Two hours of solo rowing, and then two hours of sleep in the tiny cabin in the bow. For the first week out, Danny was sick with food poisoning, and I had to be captain and in charge. It proved to us both that I could in fact pull my own weight on the water.

Once Daniel was better, we fell into a comfortable routine that bonded us together in a wonderful new partnership. Sometimes he would be sleeping so soundly that I would row for another hour or so. Often Dan would do the same—row for another hour or so and let his mum sleep. Our obvious kindness toward each other was awesome, and I found my son's kindness toward me to be overwhelming. We were a rowing team, yes, but in the larger picture we were still mother and son, loving and caring for each other unconditionally. If either of us could have given the other a full eight hours' sleep, we would have done so in a flash.

The constant rolling and heaving of the boat, the constant dampness and humidity, the lack of sleep and comfort and, of course, the heavy rowing all began to take a toll on my body that deeply worried us both. My hands were red and raw and stiff like claws. I had boils on my bottom, and I began to suffer from sciatica. There was swelling in my hip from a muscle I had torn prior to departure, and my shoulder was injured from being thrown across the boat in high seas. Danny was worried that his drive to achieve his goal was going to permanently damage his mum, and I was worried that the frailty of my fifty-three-year-old body was going to destroy my son's dream. I suddenly felt old and a burden on the venture. But then Daniel began to experience many of the same pains, and I knew it wasn't just me, but the extraordinary conditions we were living under.

Throughout the trip, there were many things that made us think about giving up. There were the hard days when we blamed each other. "How could you do this to your poor mum?" I would shout. "This is all YOUR fault!" And Daniel would yell back, "I didn't expect you to say 'Yes!'" But in truth, we decided that the only thing that would have really made us give up was if a whale had smashed our boat. Daniel laughs now and says, "And, oh my God, how many times we prayed for that!"

We were astonished as to how something as small as a rainbow or a fish leaping out of the water could instantly cheer us up when we were low. In addition, before we left, we had all our friends and relatives write poems and letters to us, and seal and date them. That way, we had mail to open on each day of our journey. The humor and love in these letters picked us up and carried us when times got really rough.

We also had on board a radar beacon that allowed us to be tracked exactly. Each night the positions of all the boats were posted on the Internet, and our friends and family were able to track us. My own sweet mum rowed the Atlantic with me every night in her dreams. My stepfather drew a map to scale on the wall, and each night friends would call and report our position to my mum. They would then plot our course on that map. In a way, it was three generations rowing the Atlantic.

Both Daniel and I took a careful selection of books and taped music along. If you think rowing the Atlantic is boring, you should try not rowing! After a while, for variety, we began to trade books and listen to each other's music. Daniel began to appreciate my classical choices, and I began to enjoy listening to his reggae and UB40!

Every team in this race had its own reasons for participating. Some were committed to winning. We, however, were doing it for the challenge and the opportunity to spend this unique time together. Knowing we would not win, we took two hours off each night, sat and enjoyed dinner, and talked. We told each other the stories and anecdotes of our lives, things that might not otherwise have been shared over a lifetime. One night over dinner I said, "This is a little bit like Scheherazade, you know, the story of *A Thousand and One Arabian Nights!*" Daniel replied, "Yes, Mum! Perhaps we should call our book *A Hundred and One Atlantic Nights!*" By complete coincidence (or was it?), that's exactly how many nights it took to cross—101!

On the night of January 22, 1998, we were approaching

Barbados, thinking we still had twenty miles to go. We were loafing, savoring the last night of our long adventure together. One last time, my son began to make me a cup of hot chocolate and turned on his headlamp for a few moments. Suddenly, the radio began to squawk. It was an escort boat, and they were looking for us. When we identified ourselves as *Carpe Diem*, we heard a lot of screaming and shouting on board: "It's them, it's them, they're safe!" They had seen Daniel's light for those few moments and were hoping it might be us. Then they told us to our shock and delight that we actually had only six miles left to go! Daniel rowed the first four and allowed me, his aching but ecstatic mum, to row the last two. I would be the one to take us across the line of longitude that was the official finish line.

To our amazement, an entire flotilla of waiting boats carrying family and friends began to cheer. They then set off fireworks, lighting up the night sky, accompanied by the triumphant cannons of the "1812 Overture" to welcome us and celebrate our safe arrival. The thrill of our accomplishment filled me in that moment, and I burst into tears and cried out, "We've done it!! Oh Daniel, we've done it!"

Because of the heavy headwind and our great fatigue, we chose to board the waiting escort boat, while our own weary little *Carpe Diem*, half filled with water and listing to one side, was towed in behind us. We were almost two months behind the winning KIWI team and thought that everyone would have forgotten about us—after all, we were the last boat in. But we were surprised and truly overwhelmed at the enormous welcome we received upon our arrival! Everyone wanted to meet and congratulate "Jan and Dan," the British mother-and-son team who had successfully rowed across the Atlantic and completed the race.

Aboard the escort boat we had an emotional reunion

with my daughter, Daniel's sister Becky. And there was one more lovely surprise! Waiting for us on shore with tears and hugs was my own sweet mum, come all the way from her home in France to welcome her jubilant daughter and grandson.

When I try and put into words what we will remember most, my journal entry from day sixty-nine speaks most poignantly of the things only my heart would know. I wrote:

> *I don't believe it is the beauty, the dolphins, whales, dawns and sunsets, although they will be with me forever. The brilliant night sky, stars, delicate new moons, brilliant full 'bright as day' moons. The power and the glory of the ocean.*
>
> *No. It is finding out how one's body and mind learn to cope. Seeing how Daniel bears up. I have found such pride in his unfailing good temper and optimism—his intrinsic kindness and thoughtfulness. I have loved the baby, the child, the boy, I have been proud of them, but now I love and admire the man, Daniel, with all my heart.*
>
> *For the rest of our lives, no matter where they may take us, we will always have the memory of this special time together, and the pride in the spectacular accomplishment that was ours, and only ours.*
>
> *We did it. Together.*

*Jan Meek with Daniel Byles*
*As told to Janet Matthews*
*Previously appeared in* Chicken Soup for the Parent's Soul

"Margo, I think we should start seeing others."

# A Miracle Between Sea and Land

Elaine Lackey has no logical explanation for an experience she shared with her son when he was lost at sea, but she cannot doubt it.

Nick Lackey's fishing boat had been sunk in a storm in the Pacific. The Coast Guard, after three days of fruitless searching, declared him presumed dead. But Elaine "had a feeling" that her son was still alive, though in grave danger.

The Thursday night after the search ended, Elaine was asleep next to her husband of forty-one years when she was awakened when, she says, her bed began to "pitch and roll as if it were being tossed about on huge waves. I literally clung to my mattress to prevent being thrown from the bed." Through it all, her husband slept undisturbed.

Elaine suddenly felt seasick, and "I knew for some inexplicable reason I was in Nick's body," she says. "I could feel his bone-weary exhaustion, his desire to give in to sleep. I knew this would mean death. So I cried out, 'Hang on, Nick! Please hang on!'"

As she felt the storm increase in intensity, Elaine, terrified, clutched the iron bars of her headboard in order to "stay afloat." She felt waves crash over the bed. Her husband finally awoke to find her coughing and spitting up water. Her face was drenched, although the bed was completely dry. As her husband held her, Elaine, still feeling buffeted by waves, again cried out, "Hang on, Nick! Hang on!"

Two days after this event, Nick Lackey was rescued by a Greek freighter. Before calling his family, he told his rescuers, "Thursday night was the worst. A new storm blew my raft all over the ocean. I was bone weary and more than once thought how easy it would be to give up and drift off to sleep. But a voice kept calling to me from somewhere: 'Hang on, Nick. Hang on.' I somehow took heart from that voice and did hang on."

Neither Nick nor Elaine can explain the events of that Thursday night. "I do believe it was my voice Nick heard," says Elaine, "but I can't imagine how that would be possible. Maybe it's just true that God works in mysterious ways."

*Alan Ebert*

*Lunar Celebration*

*Original painting by Wyland ©2003.*

# Pedaling over the Atlantic

*Ideals are like stars: You will not succeed in touching them with your hands, but like the seafaring man on the ocean desert of waters, you choose them as your guides, and following them, you reach your destiny.*

Carl Schurz

The whole crazy idea got planted in Dwight Collins's head when he was ten years old. He read (apparently missing the "KIDS: DON'T TRY THIS AT HOME" disclaimer) about two guys—Chay Blythe and John Ridgeway—who in 1966 rowed from Cape Cod to Ireland in a dory. Oars and muscles took them across the sea.

That was something Dwight could see himself doing— and not necessarily with another person.

Dwight had always liked sailing, but he started practicing with a purpose now—building and sailing rafts on the Goodwives River that ran behind his house in Noroton, Connecticut. In high school, when Dwight's friends were dreaming about fast cars or fast dates, Dwight kept a folder on solo transatlantic crossings. He stuffed it with charts, clippings and scribbled notes. He sailed and rowed and planned: He'd be the first to make a solo, self-powered trip across the Atlantic.

Later, while Dwight was a student at the University of Pennsylvania, he was flipping through an issue of *Human Power*, a publication devoted to people who think like Dwight. What if, he thought, he could bicycle across the Atlantic? With a pedal apparatus driving a propeller, his boat could have a keel, and it would be self-righting. It would be safer than rowing and far more efficient.

Rowing is an ergonomic compromise. Every pull requires a push—a motion that does nothing to propel the rower forward. Using the more powerful leg muscles, he could power the boat for hours without tiring. And—bonus!—with a pedal-powered boat, he could cover his craft. There'd be no need to have his arms sticking out into the ocean, into all those elements.

The folder grew thicker while Dwight finished college, then went on to the U.S. Navy and elite SEALS training. But when he entered the corporate world of Manhattan real estate, the dream receded in the bustle of making a living. Then, in 1987, an Englishman named Tom Mclean rowed himself across the Atlantic alone in fifty-four days. Dwight would not be the first to go solo. He put the folder away.

Real life hummed along. Dwight met Corinne Ham and got engaged. In the weeks before their wedding, Corinne was helping him move out of his apartment. "What's this, Dwight?" Corinne said one day, holding up a folder labeled "Pedal-Power Boat."

*This could be dicey,* he thought. She wasn't married to him yet. "I had this idea," he started. "I've had it for a long time, that, um, I could propel myself across the Atlantic Ocean in a pedal-powered boat."

No reaction. She was flipping through the folder.

"I could cycle to England," he added, watching her carefully.

She looked at pie charts, with their arrows and calculations, at the clippings about Tom Mclean.

"Dwight!" she said. "You've got to do this!"

"I knew then," says Dwight, "that I was engaged to the right person."

They were married June 16, 1990. Right after the wedding, they started planning the trip. Dwight hired a designer—Bruce Kirby, from Rowayton, Connecticut, the man who created the Laser design—and then a builder— Eric Goetz, of Bristol, Rhode Island, who had built America's Cup yachts. And he began to pedal.

Dwight would come home after work and get on the stationary recumbent bike they had squeezed into their tiny apartment. On her way home from work, Corinne would rent a video. While Corinne cooked dinner, Dwight pedaled. Corinne served him dinner while he pedaled. After eating, she'd pop in the movie, with the sound turned way up so he could hear it over the whirring. He stopped only to sleep. On weekends he pedaled for at least six hours a day.

There were no breaks in training. She'd say, "Hey, let's take a ride," or something, and he'd say, "Can't. Sorry, just can't." Dwight was becoming his bicycle. His thighs grew four inches.

Two years and 4,000 hours of pedaling later, Dwight was ready. His twenty-four-foot boat was equipped with solar panels to charge radio batteries, a reverse-osmosis water desalinator, his pedal station, a bunk and a camcorder he could use as a video diary. He filled the craft with dried food, books on tape (biographies of Ulysses S. Grant and J. P. Morgan), a Walkman and two dozen boxes of Fig Newtons. Next to an American flag, he hung a windsock with a shamrock on it, a gift from his father. He named the boat *Tango* after the first dance he and Corinne danced at their wedding.

On June 14, 1992, Dwight was in St. John's, Newfoundland, where a billboard boasted, "Welcome to Newfoundland. Only six motorists killed by moose this year!" Dwight decided to take it as a good omen. The weather was ready, and with his whole family and most of the puzzled local population watching, he kissed Corinne good-bye, stepped into his little kazoo-shaped boat and pedaled away.

Corinne rode behind for a while on a launch. Today, she points at the image of herself on a video taken that day. "I was trying not to cry there. You can hear it in my voice."

"I'm going to miss you," the woman in the video says. "I love you."

"Going to miss you, too," his voice came back.

For the first two weeks, Dwight pedaled an average of nineteen hours a day. He pedaled and ate; he pedaled and thought; he pedaled and listened to tapes and tried not to look at his watch; he pedaled and talked to his camcorder. Headwinds bullied him. If he stopped pedaling, he'd go backward. So he pedaled all day and went nowhere. It was like being back in the apartment. He slept an hour here, two hours there.

But the weather changed. On the radio Corinne told Dwight to expect twenty-foot seas and fifty-mile-per-hour tailwinds. One very bad storm. On the one hand, Dwight was relieved—finally, he'd have the wind on his side, pushing him forward. On the other hand, the camcorder caught him tying everything down with tiny bungee cords. "If anything happens in this water, boy," he said to the camera with a nervous laugh, "I don't know how long I'd last."

Giant waves crashed over the boat, again and again. The gale winds were pushing the little boat so hard that his pedals spun uselessly, unable to keep up with the furious propeller below. The winds howled harder. The waves towered higher. It would stay this way, a nightmare toboggan ride, sliding up and down thirty-foot waves, for four days.

When he'd been awake for two days straight, he could pedal no more. While he slept, a monster wave pitched Dwight out of his bunk and against the camcorder mounts. Then, as *Tango* righted itself, he was dumped on the deck.

His face bleeding, his eyes dazed, he asked the camcorder, "I'm not even halfway yet! What am I doing?"

When the storm subsided, he still had over twelve hundred miles of pedaling ahead of him. And he hadn't gotten any use out of the little sunroof—there had been no sun. He had serious cabin fever.

The final insult was when his Walkman stopped working. Corinne asked Sony to airdrop a replacement to him, and they liked the idea, but the weather wouldn't cooperate. Dwight resorted to building boats in his head to take his mind off the constant pedaling. He built his imaginary boat slowly, deciding with care what type of cabin and whether he wanted flush decks.

Minor mechanical problems cropped up, most of which Dwight was able to fix (except the Walkman). One was the microphone over which he talked to Corinne and his support team. The mike had gotten wet in the rough weather, and Dwight had it apart one night, trying to dry it out. "It was frustrating," he says.

"I could hear Corinne and my brother transmitting to me, but I couldn't say anything to them. I was pinching wires together, the boat was rocking, it was dark. I had the flashlight in my mouth. My brother kept saying, 'What's your problem? Over.'"

His nearest brush with humanity almost killed him.

One night, his hands full of bearings, he was working on the cycle apparatus. "All of a sudden there was a bright light. I turned around, and there was this ship coming, right in my path. I dropped the bearings. I pulled out my flares. It came at me. I turned on my radio. I turned on my light. They were literally meters away, coming at me. Then they put a spotlight on me, and they swung away."

Finally, Dwight pedaled into some nice weather. He stretched on the deck and put his face in the sun. Corinne contacted the local wire service in Plymouth, England, and told them to expect a visitor shortly. They broke the story. "There's a bloody wally bicycling across the pond!" the Coast Guard announced. The BBC sent helicopters out to report his progress. The *Daily Mirror* posed the question: "WHAT MAKES A MAN BATTLE 2,200 MILES ALONE ACROSS THE SEA IN A PEDAL BOAT?" Their answer: "Because Dwight is obsessed with the call of the wild . . . he cannot face life without proving his manhood . . . and that means staring danger and death in the face." *Sheesh,* Dwight thought later when he read it.

On day thirty-nine—a beautiful day—he spotted the Scilly Islands at the southwestern tip of England. "I wouldn't trade this for the world," he said to the camcorder.

The next day, July 24, 1992, Dwight pedaled *Tango* into Plymouth Harbor, 2,250 miles from St. John's. He had broken the record for the fastest human-powered Atlantic crossing by fourteen days.

"As I came around the bend," he recalls, "there was a huge crowd of people, and everybody was clapping. My whole family was on the deck."

Dwight pedaled up to the dock, and Corinne fell onto the boat, into his arms, though surely she must have been tempted to embrace his legs, which got him there.

Looking back now, Dwight admits that, yes, challenging

yourself like this can be addictive, but he certainly can resist it. "This was just a thing that I wanted to do," he says with finality. He's done with such things as pedaling across the ocean.

Although, he does have another idea . . .

*Jamie Kageleiry*

# Fear of the Unknown

"I'm going to try out to be a Laguna Beach ocean lifeguard, Mom," Malea announced one winter day. She was a freshman at UCLA, home for the weekend.

"Wow, that's great," I said, hiding my apprehension. It sounded dangerous to me, but my daughter had always been a brave soul with a big heart, fierce focus and mighty determination. I had no doubt she would succeed at whatever she tackled.

"What does trying out involve?" I asked.

"Just some weekend training sessions," she said, "then a tryout day." She always made everything sound easy. "I'll come home from school every weekend until it's over."

I quickly learned that my daughter's definition of easy was very different from mine. Those weekend sessions were grueling—for both of us. Malea was no stranger to strenuous training, having been on the cross-country team and the swim team in high school, but neither of us had experienced anything like ocean lifeguard training.

Beginning in mid-March, she spent hours each weekend with the other contestants running up and down the beaches, up and down the stairs, and in and out of the chilly winter waters of the Pacific. It was physically painful and emotionally draining. Her feet blistered, and her muscles ached. Sometimes I would stand on the beach and watch her struggle to keep up with the rest, struggle to finish, struggle to keep from giving up. It made both of us cry. Hers were tears of exhaustion and frustration with her own physical limitations. My tears were a heart-wrenching mixture of pride and agony from watching her push herself beyond her limitations and beyond the pain. We longed for it to be over.

The night before the tryout, we sat together talking about the big day ahead. While it never occurred to me that she wouldn't make it, I was surprised to find that she had her doubts. Something else was bothering her, something that she seemed reluctant to reveal even to me.

"Everyone else is so much stronger and faster than I am," she said.

"It's not always about stronger and faster," I said, attempting to bolster her sagging confidence. "Sometimes sheer grit and determination will push you to the top. You've got heart, Malea. I know you'll be right in there with the best of them."

"It's not just that."

"Well, what else then?" I said. "It's just you pushing yourself to do your very best. When you boil it all down, that's all you have to worry about."

"No," she said quietly, her head bowed, hands clenched in her lap. "That's not everything. . . . Mom, I'm afraid of sharks."

"What do you mean?" I asked, puzzled. "What do sharks have to do with it?"

That's when I found out that her final challenge would be to make her way alone on a giant paddleboard to a buoy just beyond the horizon, about one thousand yards offshore. Definitely potential shark territory. Once at the designated spot, she would lower herself into the water, swim about two hundred feet from the safety of the paddle-board, circle the board and swim back to it. Once back on the paddleboard, she had to stand up and shout a procla-mation to the world. Only then could she return to shore.

All of the participants had been given the same instruc-tions, and I wondered if they were afraid of sharks, too. I imagine most people harbor a deep fear of the fierce ocean predator. Malea's anxiety was no different, I suppose, but the whole idea of facing her fear to complete the exercise was overwhelming. I could see she seriously questioned her ability to meet the challenge.

My daughter and I are not quitters, but at that moment I wanted to wrap her in my arms and tell her it was okay, that being an ocean lifeguard wasn't all it was cracked up to be. Couldn't she just work at the Juice Stop this sum-mer? Or some other nice, safe job? Instead, I took her hands in mine and said, "You can do it, Malea." But I was scared to death for her.

The next morning was unusually cold, dreary and damp. Standing on the wet sand, I could barely see the ocean before me as all the kids stripped to their swimsuits and prepared for competition. The running, swimming, more running and more swimming portion of the tryout took several hours. I spent those hours with the rest of the anxious parents, wrapped warmly in my sweatshirt, sit-ting on the beach, trying to see through the fog. As each event ended, my daughter and I calculated her position amongst her peers. Then it was time for the final chal-lenge. We sat on the shore waiting her turn, and Malea was quiet, working solemnly on her courage. I could see her struggling to find her focus. Finally, it was her turn, and as she approached the water's edge, I felt myself los-ing my emotional grip. My heart was firmly planted in my throat. As she disappeared into the soupy, cold atmo-sphere, I held my breath.

I strained to see her, but I couldn't make out a thing beyond the shoreline. Maybe that was a blessing. I would only have seen her swim out of range, past the horizon and into lonely, scary, black waters—shark waters. It felt as though I sat on that cold, wet sand for hours, barely breathing, heart pounding. When I thought I was going to burst, that I just could not stand it one minute longer, I saw the faint outline of the giant paddleboard emerge from the haze. Malea straddled it proudly and firmly, sporting a look on her face that comes only from having pushed oneself beyond all expectation. I ran to the paddleboard, grabbed my daughter and hugged her, both of us awash in tears as we held each other.

"I did it!" she cried. "I did it!"

I was so proud of her accomplishment. Not only had she successfully completed the training and now the try-out, but she had conquered her fears. Sheer grit and determination had paid off. After paddling out beyond the safety of the shore and swimming alone in the dark ocean, Malea got up on the paddleboard and shouted her proclamation to the world . . .

"I . . . AM NOT . . . AFRAID . . . OF SHARKS!"

*Maggie Stapp-Hempen*

# Exploring the Sunken Wreck

We were about to take our first close look at the mighty *Bismarck*, unseen by human eyes for almost fifty years. Billy Yunck's watch was on duty in the control van, and there were quite a few spectators. No one who was awake wanted to miss the show.

"All right, let's see what kind of shape she's in," I said. "Billy, go down slowly."

Billy pushed forward on the joystick, and the altitude reading began to decrease: fifty meters, forty-five meters, forty meters, thirty-five meters.

We were coming in directly over the wreck, like a helicopter dropping down over an enemy position. About thirty meters from the bottom, a ghostly gray form materialized dimly in the murky distance.

"Okay, bring her down gently." The wind on the surface had been picking up for the past couple of hours, and *Argo*, our deep-sea exploration vessel, was rising and falling as much as several meters with each swell. The last thing I needed right now was a crash landing.

Gradually, the murk thinned, and the detail of the picture on the video monitors came into focus. First we saw an undamaged gun turret, then horribly mangled metal plating where a shell had hit.

Our goal was to videotape and photograph every inch of the sunken ship. As the hours passed, a clearer picture of the wreck began to emerge. It was a strange mixture of destruction and preservation. Many guns were still in place, but there were some huge holes in the deck, and some of the upper parts of the ship had been completely blasted away.

At 4 P.M. sharp, Todd's watch relieved Billy's. In the three hours that we'd been working over the wreck, the surface weather had been getting steadily worse, and the flyer's job was becoming more difficult by the minute. But Todd was an expert at counteracting the rise and fall of our ship, the *Star Hercules*. As the ship fell, he raised *Argo*; as it rose, he lowered it. This worked well until we hit a deep trough between waves where the ship fell and then fell further, instead of going up again. A few times we come close to crashing.

As we approached the rear gunnery control station, I sensed an extra level of anticipation in the can. We had all read the *Bismarck* story, and we knew that this was where Lieutenant-Commander Burkard von Mullenhim-Rechberg had spent the battle. This was also the place where so many of those who survived the sinking had sought shelter, including the three friends from the rear gunnery computer room—Adi Eich, Franz Halke and Heinz Jucknat.

The station was intact. It was amazing that it had survived the battle so well, since it was not a heavily armored structure.

Now we headed aft, past the round, gaping mouths where turrets Caesar and Dora had once sat. None of the four big turrets was still attached to the ship. Soon we were out over empty decking and approaching the stern.

"Stop! What's that?" I said. *Argo*'s video cameras had just picked up some dark markings on the ship.

"It's a cross," said a voice behind me.

"No," I said, looking intently at the screen. "No, that's not a cross. It's a swastika."

"Of course, the swastika!" exclaimed Hagen, half to himself.

The van went silent. In our excitement we'd forgotten just what we were looking at: a Nazi warship. Suddenly, all the evil associations that went with the Nazi symbol ran through our minds: the invasions that led to the outbreak of World War II, bringing widespread death and destruction, the concentration camps and the millions of people murdered there. My mind went back to the day Hitler came on board to inspect his new battleship before her first mission. I wondered how differently the war might have turned out if the *Bismarck* had broken into the Atlantic to attack ships transporting food and supplies to the islands of Great Britain.

Although the swastikas on the bow and stern decks had been painted over, after forty-eight years the seawater had gradually worn that paint away. As we moved further aft, the swastika suddenly sheared away as if chopped by a guillotine.

"That took one heck of a karate chop," I said.

"Wow!" said Todd. "Do you think that was caused by a torpedo?"

"If so, no one saw it happen when the ship was still at the surface," I replied.

As we moved off the stern, we glimpsed rubble down below, but there was no sign of the vanished chunk of hull.

For almost five hours we beetled our way along the deck of the ravaged ship, awed by the damage yet marveling at how much remained and what the survivors would think when they saw the pictures of the *Bismarck* again after so long.

## June 12, 1989

"Being gathered here today gives us the opportunity to remember those young British and German seamen who lost their lives during the days of this tragic sea battle . . ."

The stern deck of the *Star Hercules* was crowded with people. Almost everyone on board had turned out for a memorial service organized by Hagen Schempf and conducted by the captain of the *Star Hercules*. The weather was beautiful—bright, warm sun and a gentle wind. The storm that had made our last days on site so difficult was now a distant memory.

I looked around the deck. The officers were in their dress uniforms, and the rest of us had done our best to make ourselves presentable, but we were a motley crew: During our weeks at sea, beards had gone unshaven, hair uncut. Todd and his friends stood together, listening quietly.

". . . let us hope that this kind of human suffering and sacrifice may never be asked of mankind again."

The captain called for a minute of silence. I glanced over at Hagen and wondered what he was thinking. Finding the wreck had brought him face to face with a piece of his own history. He didn't talk about it, but it was obvious to anyone who knew him well that he had been deeply affected by the experience.

In the silence the only sounds were the wind, the throbbing of the ship's engines and the cry of seabirds. As I stood with my head bowed, I remembered another shipboard service that had taken place forty-eight years earlier, aboard the *Dorsetshire*. I imagined I could hear the plaintive strains of the German sailors' lament "I had a comrade" as a flag-draped body disappeared into the sea.

*Dr. Robert D. Ballard*

# Using His Teeth

During World War II, a young Navy lieutenant was on patrol duty in the Solomon Islands, northeast of Australia in the South Pacific. His name was John F. Kennedy.

Kennedy commanded a small-motor torpedo boat, the PT–109, and the boat's twelve-man crew. Their mission: to observe and report the movements of Japanese warships.

Shortly after midnight on August 2, 1943, a Japanese destroyer loomed suddenly out of a fog. It crashed into Kennedy's boat, plunging all aboard into the ocean.

Two crewmen died. The others clung to the wreckage all night long. As dawn broke, Kennedy ordered: "Swim to that island!" It was no easy task. The island seemed near, but was actually miles away.

The men began swimming, but one, seriously hurt, could not. The skipper had an idea. Despite his own injured back, Kennedy grasped the strap of a life belt in his strong teeth. With the seaman attached to the other end, Kennedy swam for four hours to the island.

That was clever, but more ingenuity was to come. Kennedy carved a message for help on a coconut shell and had a young islander take it to the nearest base. The message got through. On August 7, help arrived.

Seventeen years later, Kennedy was elected America's thirty-fifth president. He kept the coconut shell in the Oval Office of the White House.

*Lester David*
Boys' Life *magazine*

*Reach for Stars*

*Original painting by Wyland ©2003.*

# 8

# SAVING THE SEA

*For most of history, man has had to fight nature to survive; in this century he is beginning to realize that, in order to survive, he must protect it.*

Jacques Cousteau

# This Magic Moment

*If there is magic on the planet, it is contained in the water.*

Loren Eisley

It was like many Maui mornings, the sun rising over Haleakala as we greeted our divers for the day's charter. As my captain and I explained the dive procedures, I noticed the wind line moving into Molokini, a small, crescent-shaped island that harbors a large reef. I slid through the briefing, then prompted my divers to gear up, careful to do everything right so the divers would feel confident with me, the dive leader.

The dive went pretty close to how I had described it: The garden eels performed their underwater ballet, the parrot fish grazed on the coral, and the ever-elusive male flame wrasse flared their colors to defend their territory. Near the last level of the dive, two couples in my group signaled they were going to ascend. As luck would have it, the remaining divers were two European brothers, who were obviously troubled by the idea of a "woman" dive master and had ignored me for the entire dive.

The three of us caught the current and drifted along the outside of the reef, slowly beginning our ascent until, far below, something caught my eye. After a few moments, I made out the white shoulder patches of a manta ray in about one hundred and twenty feet of water.

Manta rays are one of my greatest loves, but very little is known about them. They feed on plankton, which makes them more delicate than an aquarium can handle. They travel the oceans and are therefore a mystery.

Mantas can be identified by the distinctive pattern on their belly, with no two rays alike. In 1992, I had been identifying the manta rays that were seen at Molokini and found that some were known, but many more were sighted only once, and then gone.

So there I was: a beautiful, very large ray beneath me and my skeptical divers behind. I reminded myself that I was still trying to win their confidence, and a bounce to see this manta wouldn't help my case. So I started calling through my regulator, "Hey, come up and see me!" I had tried this before to attract the attention of whales and dolphins, who are very chatty underwater and will come sometimes just to see what the noise is about. My divers were just as puzzled by my actions, but continued to try to ignore me.

There was another dive group ahead of us. The leader, who was a friend of mine and knew me to be fairly sane, stopped to see what I was doing. I kept calling to the ray, and when she shifted in the water column, I took that as a sign that she was curious. So I started waving my arms, calling her up to me.

After a minute, she lifted away from where she had been riding the current and began to make a wide circular glide until she was closer to me. I kept watching as she slowly moved back and forth, rising higher, until she was directly beneath the two Europeans and me. I looked at them and was pleased to see them smiling. Now they liked me. After all, I could call up a manta ray!

Looking back to the ray, I realized she was much bigger than what we were used to around Molokini—a good fifteen feet from wing tip to wing tip, and not a familiar-looking ray. I had not seen this animal before. There was something else odd about her. I just couldn't figure out what it was.

Once my brain clicked in and I was able to concentrate, I saw deep V-shaped marks of her flesh missing from her backside. Other marks ran up and down her body. At first I thought a boat had hit her. As she came closer, now with only ten feet separating us, I realized what was wrong.

She had fishing hooks embedded in her head by her eye, with very thick fishing line running to her tail. She had rolled with the line and was wrapped head to tail about five or six times. The line had torn into her body at the back, and those were the V-shaped chunks that were missing.

I felt sick and, for a moment, paralyzed. I knew wild animals in pain would never tolerate a human to inflict more pain. But I had to do something.

Forgetting about my air, my divers and where I was, I went to the manta. I moved very slowly and talked to her the whole time, like she was one of the horses I had grown up with. When I touched her, her whole body quivered, like my horse would. I put both of my hands on her, then my entire body, talking to her the whole time. I knew that she could knock me off at any time with one flick of her great wing.

When she had steadied, I took out the knife that I carry on my inflator hose and lifted one of the lines. It was tight and difficult to get my finger under, almost like a guitar string. She shook, which told me to be gentle. It was obvious that the slightest pressure was painful.

As I cut through the first line, it pulled into her wounds. With one beat of her mighty wings, she dumped me and bolted away. I figured that she was gone and was amazed when she turned and came right back to me, gliding under my body. I went to work. She seemed to know it would hurt, and somehow, she also knew that I could help. Imagine the intelligence of that creature, to come for help and to trust!

I cut through one line and into the next until she had all she could take of me and would move away, only to return in a moment or two. I never chased her. I would never chase any animal. I never grabbed her. I allowed her to be in charge, and she always came back.

When all the lines were cut on top, on her next pass, I went under her to pull the lines through the wounds at the back of her body. The tissue had started to grow around them, and they were difficult to get loose. I held myself against her body, with my hand on her lower jaw. She held as motionless as she could. When it was all loose, I let her go and watched her swim in a circle. She could have gone then, and it would have all fallen away. She came back, and I went back on top of her.

The fishing hooks were still in her. One was barely hanging on, which I removed easily. The other was buried by her eye at least two inches past the barb. Carefully, I began to take it out, hoping I wasn't damaging anything. She did open and close her eye while I worked on her, and finally, it was out. I held the hooks in one hand, while I gathered the fishing line in the other hand, my weight on the manta.

I could have stayed there forever! I was totally oblivious to everything but that moment. I loved this manta. I was so moved that she would allow me to do this to her. But reality came screaming down on me. With my air running out, I reluctantly came to my senses and pushed myself away.

At first, she stayed below me. And then, when she realized that she was free, she came to life like I never would have imagined she could. I thought she was sick and weak, since her mouth had been tied closed, and she hadn't been able to feed for however long the lines had been on her. I thought wrong! With two beats of those powerful wings, she rocketed along the wall of Molokini and then directly out to sea! I lost view of her and, remembering my divers, turned to look for them.

Remarkably, we hadn't traveled very far. My divers were right above me and had witnessed the whole event, thankfully! No one would have believed me alone. It seemed too amazing to have really happened. But as I looked at the hooks and line in my hands and felt the torn calluses from her rough skin, I knew that, yes, it really had happened.

I kicked in the direction of my divers, whose eyes were still wide from the encounter, only to have them signal me to stop and turn around. Until this moment, the whole experience had been phenomenal, but I could explain it. Now, the moment turned magical.

I turned and saw her slowly gliding toward me. With barely an effort, she approached me and stopped, her wing just touching my head. I looked into her round, dark eye, and she looked deeply into me. I felt a rush of something that so overpowered me, I have yet to find the words to describe it, except a warm and loving flow of energy from her into me.

She stayed with me for a moment. I don't know if it was a second or an hour. Then, as sweetly as she came back, she lifted her wing over my head and was gone. A manta thank-you.

I hung in midwater, using the safety-stop excuse, and tried to make sense of what I had experienced. Eventually, collecting myself, I surfaced and was greeted by an ecstatic group of divers and a curious captain. They all gave me time to get my heart started and to begin to breathe.

Sadly, I have not seen her since that day, and I am still looking. For the longest time, though my wetsuit was tattered and torn, I would not change it because I thought she wouldn't recognize me. I call to every manta I see, and they almost always acknowledge me in some way. One day, though, it will be her. She'll hear me and pause, remembering the giant cleaner that she trusted to relieve her pain, and she'll come. At least that is how it happens in my dreams.

*Jennifer Anderson*

# A New Dawn for Whaling in Taiji

Whaling in Japan goes back to prehistoric times, when villagers along the coast would butcher dead whales that washed up from the sea. An old Japanese proverb says, "A whale on the beach is wealth for seven villages."

In 1606, Japanese whalers went out and killed their first great whale. Working from tiny boats, using nets and hand-thrown harpoons, they were like Cro-Magnon men taking down a mastadon.

Later in the same century, whales became scarce in Japanese coastal waters because of the industrial whaling of the Americans and Europeans offshore. Japanese whalers borrowed their competitors' techniques and expanded into large-scale whaling. During the 1940s, facing food shortages during and after World War II, the Japanese turned to whale meat to fill their diet.

During the early post-war years, the International Whaling Commission was formed to address the depletion of the whale populations. At the same time, new technologies made it possible to study whales in their habitat, to learn their social structures and to hear their songs echoing across the deep.

Conservationists began to protest the killing of the

whales, and one by one, the world's nations stopped whaling, with Japan remaining as one of the few holdouts.

Throughout these centuries, Taiji, a little town on the southern coast of Japan, has occupied a central place in the whaling story. It was from Taiji, in 1675, that Japan's first large-scale, organized whaling expedition was launched. Even now, more than 90 percent of the town's people work in the whaling industry, and they see whale hunting as part of their cultural heritage. The ongoing slaughter has brought whaling, and specifically Taiji whaling, under attack.

Into this charged climate, in the mid-1980s, Taiji's town leaders invited me to their community. They hoped that an artist, even a whale-loving artist, would listen to their concerns about what they saw as the destruction of their heritage. If I could hear them out, they thought, I might help turn aside the international criticism directed against them.

I walked through this beautiful little town, perched on steep, forested hillsides and surrounded by the sea. Out in the bay was a lot of activity.

A small fleet of fishing boats, working in tandem, closed a gap in a bay just below the town hall. I knew enough about Taiji's whaling methods to guess what I was seeing, but I had to ask.

I was right. What I was seeing was a group of whalers herding a pod of pilot whales into the tiny bay. When they finished the roundup, they would secure a net across the opening of the bay and then slaughter the whales the next day.

Pilot whales travel in groups of as many as fifty, and the kind of kill I was seeing can wipe out a whole generation, along with the young. It's hard for the whales to come back from that kind of devastation.

All through the discussions with the mayor and the town officials, I kept thinking about what was going on outside the window. They said that even though they killed the whales, they still honored and respected them.

I told them that whale watching is taking hold in other countries, and it's becoming a bigger industry than whaling ever was. Taiji's officials were open to that, but they still wanted to hang on to their tradition of hunting.

The town officials took me out to show me around. We walked around the bay, where the whales broke the surface of the water and disappeared, while the whalers shouted from boat to boat, coordinating their movements as they set the net in place.

On down the cove was the town whaling museum, decorated with a tile mural of a right whale. It wasn't bad, but it was abstract, and it didn't bring the viewer any closer to what the whale really is. But the museum had a big blank wall that would be perfect for a mural. I talked to the officials about what I could do with that wall. I knew that if I could paint a wall there, it would show living whales as an object of beauty and not just a commercial product.

The officials liked the idea, and when I left, I truly respected them, but I couldn't stop thinking about the whales and the herding boats. I was going to catch a plane the next morning, and I tried to put the scene out of my mind and sleep.

I woke with a start sometime after midnight, knowing that I had to do something. I shook awake Kevin Short, my translator and traveling companion, an American who worked for the *Japan Times*. I told him, "We've got to go down and help those whales." Kevin and a Canadian photographer who was traveling with us and I all went down to the cove.

We stood on the rocks beside the bay, listening to the waves lapping against the beach. By a sliver of moonlight, we could see the thirty adult whales circled protectively around the big dominant male. It was a very spiritual thing to see these animals, so peaceful and harmless, so vulnerable. What kept ringing in my mind was that the next morning they were going to be cut up and sent to restaurants all over Japan. As we watched, the whales would surface at times, clearing their blowholes with a wet sigh.

When I went down to the water, I didn't know what I intended to do. I didn't go to that town to be a radical. I had earned the respect of the fishermen and had met the mayor, and I had an invitation to create a mural in their town. Yet as my mind constructed the gory slaughter of the next morning, I had no choice but to go into the water. I took all my clothes off, down to my BVDs, dove in and swam with those whales.

At first, the whole pod drew back from me. But then the group opened up and invited me inside its circle, letting me swim in their midst. One whale actually pushed me toward the net, knowing that I had hands and could help them. As I moved toward the net, carried by the force of the whale's nudge and this inner compulsion, I saw a baby with its mother. Whale calves are rare, and it was wrenching to know that even if this baby survived tomorrow's slaughter, it would not survive the loss of its mother.

I found myself at the opening of the bay with my hands on the imprisoning net. I began to untie it.

Kevin Short had lived in Japan for fifteen years, had found a place in Japanese culture, and understood and respected Japanese ways. When he saw what I was doing, he dove into the water and physically dragged me away from the net.

"What are you doing?" Kevin shouted.

"I can't bear to see these whales being killed," I said, shaking loose from his grip.

"You know, Wyland," Kevin came back, "that's a great, noble thing you want to do, but if you do that, you will set what you have tried to do back fifty years."

Dawn had begun to color the eastern sky, and at the horizon of audibility was the hum of the whaling-boat engines.

"You've already painted one Whaling Wall in Japan," Kevin continued. He was in the water, standing between me and the net. I didn't want to listen to him, but he just kept talking. "People are beginning to understand the living whale because of your work, because of the power of your art. If you do this, you'll kill the very thing that you've set out to do."

The sun came up, and the whaleboats began to come in. I could have released the whales. I'd have gotten arrested, but that didn't bother me. What stopped me was that I now had a chance to paint a mural that the townspeople would see every day, a chance that would be gone if I untied the rope.

The question came down to this: Do I try to save these thirty whales, which the whalers would probably have herded up again anyway, or do I continue to paint murals on public walls and museums and inspire people in a positive way?

As I scrambled out of the water and got into my clothes, I tried not to see the whalers loading up their harpoon guns. But I couldn't hide from my own sense of betrayal. I was torn apart inside, and on the train back to Tokyo, I cried with grief, rage and frustration.

The guilt stays with me today. It's terrible to think about the slaughter, but I know Kevin Short was right.

I did go back the next year and paint a mural on the wall of Taiji's whaling museum. A fisherman there told me it was the first time he had seen a living whale swimming. Before that, he had thought of whales only as dead meat.

The Japanese find the whales' eyes on the mural very powerful, especially the right whale, which makes eye contact with every passerby.

After many years and four Whaling Walls in Japan, whale watching is beginning to take hold there. Young people are turning against whaling, looking for their heritage somewhere else, and calling for an end to whaling in Japan. We may be seeing a new dawn for the whales of Japan.

*Wyland*

# Fighting for Their Lives

*Great things are done when men and mountains meet.*

William Blake

In my nightmares I saw the lifeless bodies of marine mammals washing up on shore. Our nonprofit organization, Save the Whales, was trying to prevent the United States Navy from performing "ship shock" tests in the Channel Islands Marine Sanctuary, a biologically sensitive area off the coast of California. The waters were home to endangered blue, sperm, fin and humpback whales, as well as dolphins, seals and sea lions. If the navy went ahead with its plan to test the hull integrity of its new cruisers by detonating 270 underwater explosives—some as large as 10,000 pounds—over the next five years, hundreds of thousands of these beautiful animals would die. The detonations would kill many animals outright. Others would face a slow lingering death from damage to their internal organs and hearing.

As time went on, we were joined at public hearings by numerous organizations, celebrities, scientists and citizens who agreed that the navy's testing proposal didn't ensure the safety of the marine mammals around the Channel Islands. All of these written statements were supposed to be taken into account before the federal agency in charge of marine mammal protection made a decision. After the last hearing I asked an agent when we could expect a decision. He told me to call the next week, but something in his voice seemed to imply that a decision had already been made.

"What do you mean by that?" I asked him.

He smirked. "I can't discuss it."

That expression, that we didn't stand a chance against the government, infuriated me. When I told him I would see him in court, he started laughing, as if I had made the most ludicrous statement in history. His reaction was just another example of the uphill battles we faced.

Our legal team had managed to arrange a few meetings with naval officials. Each time we asked the navy to consider alternate tests in areas less populated with marine mammals. On the day our last request was refused, I joined my mother for dinner. Neither of us felt like eating. "What else can we do?" my mother said. She had supported me throughout this fight against the government, and I could see that it had taken its toll on her. No one had ever stopped the navy from performing these kinds of tests before. Even other environmental organizations said that it was hopeless. "You will never stop the navy!" they said. I always replied, "How will you ever know if you don't have the courage to try?"

But we were running out of time.

The first test was scheduled in less than a month. Our legal case to block the tests required the declaration of an expert scientist in the marine mammal field who specialized in bioacoustics. All of the experts we contacted were unwilling to speak out against the testing because their research was funded by the U.S. government. "We need to find an expert independent of government funding," I told my mom. She looked skeptical. "We've tried everyone in the country," she said. "Who else is there?"

The answer came from Paul Spong, Ph.D., in British Columbia. Dr. Spong told me that we had no other option than to look outside the United States.

I cried, "I can do that?"

"An expert is an expert," he replied.

With less than two weeks before testing began, Hal Whitehead, Ph.D., a Canadian, and the world's foremost authority on sperm whales, agreed to testify. His testimony revealed in gripping detail how the naval tests would deprive these marine mammals of the very senses they depended on to survive in the wild. Soon other experts joined the struggle. The hearing lasted five days. At its conclusion, the presiding judge, Stephen V. Wilson of the United States District Court, Central District, ruled in our favor. He said that the navy had failed in its obligation to protect marine mammals, that it hadn't prepared a full environmental impact statement, and that it hadn't investigated all reasonable alternative sites and properly mitigated the impact of detonations on marine life. The exception was that one detonation would be allowed farther offshore with observers, of our choice, and instruments to help detect deep-diving marine mammals.

Those of us who had fought so long and hard listened to Judge Wilson with a mixture of disbelief and elation. A handful of people had achieved the impossible. We had taken on the mightiest naval force in the history of the world—and we had won! We prevented 269 naval detonations, and in so doing, saved the lives of more than 10,000 marine mammals.

*Maris Sidenstecker*

*Dolphin Rides*

*Original painting by Wyland ©2003.*

# Everything I Needed to Know About the Ocean I Learned in the Second Grade

*Filthy water cannot be washed.*

African Proverb

Every time I meet with a group of kids, I'm reminded of why I and so many other people work so hard to preserve the beauty of our natural world. Mention the ocean to children, and their eyes light up. Ask them about whales or dolphins or sea turtles and you'll get a joyful litany of facts, figures and explanations. Children accept our world unconditionally. When they're happy, it shows. When they're dissatisfied with the state of things, they'll let you know. I got a glimpse of this recently during a visit to a second-grade class in Southern California. I was lucky enough to talk with a group of bright, funny kids right after they had taken part in a cleanup project at a nearby beach. Even at seven years old, the kids were learning how important it is to become caretakers for the environment.

Being a curious person, I wanted to hear what they

learned from their recent experience. My "panel" included Johnny, Cassidy, Sarah F. and Sarah G., Matt and Jenna—all bubbling at the idea of sharing their thoughts.

First we had to decide who would answer my questions. Sarah G., the most outgoing of the group, thought the first person who slammed their hand down on the table, "like they do in *Family Feud*," should be given the honor of responding. We tried this a few times, and then moved on to the more democratic approach of taking turns. With the new ground rules firmly in place—for the time being, anyway—I asked the group to start the discussion by naming a few different types of bodies of water. The answers came fast and furious: "The ocean!" "A river!" "Lakes!" "Streams!" "Ponds!" . . . "Fresno!"

The last answer came from Matt.

"Fresno?" I asked.

"Fresno has water," he said, proudly.

I couldn't argue with his logic. Fresno does have water. I'm pretty sure of that.

I could see I was in good hands. Clearly, this was an advanced group. So I upped the ante and moved in with a real hardball question. Pollution is something that I often talk about when I meet with kids. They have very strong opinions on the subject and, in fact, they can be very persuasive in encouraging adults to curtail environmentally damaging habits. All it takes is one withering look from a little kid to make you pick up your chewing-gum wrappers for the rest of your life.

"How can adults take more responsibility for the environment?" I asked.

Cassidy's hand shot up.

"Don't litter," she said. "And don't waste water. . . . I turn off the water when I'm brushing my teeth."

Yes, I said, that's important. I tried to remember if I had turned off my faucet that morning. I imagined the lecture these guys would give me if I had left the water running. Next we talked about the types of trash they saw during their beach cleanup experience. Apparently, the beach that day was littered with plastic water bottles, Styrofoam, grocery bags, cigarette butts and beer cans. The kids asked me how adults could be so forgetful.

"That trash washes out to sea," Johnny said. "Fish eat it."

"But they don't like it," Jenna said. "If I were a dolphin and saw someone dropping trash in my home, I'd think that's not fair."

Sarah F. said, "When a dolphin sees trash, it probably wants to swim away to someplace cleaner . . . probably farther out to sea where we'll never get to see it again."

I asked if any of them had seen really polluted water. The answers were a mixture of yeses and noes. Matt, who judging by his T-shirt was an active member of the Indian Guides, said he'd seen a dirty lake in Idaho. He said the water was hard to see through. "It's kind of smoky looking . . . and it smells," he said.

When I asked what dirty water smells like, Sarah G. said, "Polluted water smells like dirty socks." She volunteered to take off her shoes to demonstrate.

I told her I got the point.

*Wyland*

# Do You Hear It?

The ocean is breathing, do you hear it?
Its soft breath rolls with every wave.
It crashes upon the sandy beach
Making its mark upon the shore.

The ocean is whispering, do you hear it?
Its soft voice is a melody of the wind across the water.
It whistles silently through our minds
Making its mark upon our souls.

The ocean is calling, do you hear it?
The sweet sound of life beneath.
It calls to you, it calls to me
Making its mark upon our hearts.

The ocean is weeping, do you hear it?
The silent cries rise from the deep.
It pleads for us to save it
Making its mark upon our conscience.

Will you help it? Do you hear it?
The voice so sweet and gentle.
All it asks is that you help
And keep its breath safe from harm.

*Tiffany Pope, age 16*

# Life Imitates Art

*No one person has to do it all, but if each one of us follows our heart and our own inclinations, we will find the small things that we can do to create a sustainable future and a healthy environment.*

John Denver

I'm constantly amazed at the goodwill and support of the many people who turn out to watch me paint my murals. Of course, at the same time, there's always at least one critic in the crowd. My mural in the small community of Marathon in the Florida Keys was one such experience. Painted on a building along the A1A Highway, the mural I wanted to create was to be over 150 feet long and twenty feet high, making it the largest in Southern Florida, not to mention a landmark for many years to come. For me there was no pressure. I would simply paint the undersea world of Florida's colorful living reefs, then add a life-size sperm whale and her calf. Finally, I intended to paint all the different kinds of marine life that thrived in the warm tropical waters around the keys.

As expected, the mural generated a lot of attention. Thousands of people showed up to watch its evolution. On the last day I decided to paint a large green sea turtle hovering over the reef. I didn't have any photographs of a green sea turtle, but I had a great deal of experience swimming with them in Hawaii, Florida and other parts of the world, so I winged it from memory. As I was completing the turtle, a local marine biologist approached me in a huff and told me point-blank: "That is not a green sea turtle." Naturally, this surprised me. So I asked him politely what he thought it was. He took a step forward, peered at me above his glasses and said in a scolding voice, "It's a combination of a hawksbill turtle and a green sea turtle . . . there is no such thing." I tried to defend myself with artistic license and all, but he was adamant about critiquing every aspect of this imaginary species. He seemed very upset that I could even do this without his permission and finally left in disgust. All I could do was shrug and say, "Hey, I did the best I could."

The new mural was dedicated the next day at a special ceremony. The entire town showed up to cheer their new landmark and the environmental message that it carried. Ten years passed. One afternoon I received a phone call at my home studio in Hawaii from my good friend Mandy Rodriguez, the vice president of Dolphin Research Center in Grassy Key, Florida. Mandy seemed very excited. "Hey, Wyland," he said, "you're not going to believe this. I just got a call from the turtle hospital in Marathon. They just saved a sick little hawksbill green sea turtle." He paused to catch his breath. "That's a species that no one's ever seen before! The first thing I thought of when I heard about it was you. They want you to come down next month and release the turtle into the Atlantic Ocean."

I was amazed to hear this news, and I had to admit I had a huge smirk on my face, remembering the words of the turtle expert at the mural site. I was pretty used to the idea of art imitating life, but I never thought I'd see the day when life would imitate art. Mandy explained that the turtle owed its survival to the turtle hospital in Marathon, where they perform rescues of turtles all over Florida—the first facility of its kind. The volunteers at the hospital include doctors who actually perform surgery on injured turtles and remove the life-threatening tumors that are being found more and more on these endangered creatures. The general feeling is that pesticides and other chemicals are entering the food chain and the turtles, which have thrived for 200 million years, are feeling the full impact of man's destruction of the ocean environment. Every once in a while, though, there is a victory, as in the case of this young hawksbill green sea turtle. It had been found stranded on the beach, dying from malnutrition. Soon it was to be returned, healthy and recuperated, back into the sea.

When I flew down to Marathon to see this amazing new species I was astounded. It was exactly like I had pictured it. I hate to personify animals, but this turtle was one of the cutest things I had ever seen. As I gazed at the turtle, I was amazed that, sure enough, it had the features of both the green sea turtle and the hawksbill. Nature never fails to astonish me, and I felt like this was an important moment in science and art. Gently, I lifted the fragile, five-inch creature from its healing tank and carried it to the fishing boat of Richie Moretti, the founder of the turtle hospital. Mandy Rodriquez joined us, and we boated out to sea in search of the sea-grass cover that would camouflage and protect the turtle until it was large enough to defend itself.

Eventually, we found a large, thick floating mass of sea grass—the perfect place to release the turtle. The boat stopped and, carefully, I slipped into the Atlantic with the turtle in my hand, placing it near the edge of the sea grass. To my surprise, it circled around to me and hovered by my face mask before disappearing into the sea grass. To this day I believe there was something miraculous about the entire event. It shows that we do not know all the mysteries of the sea, that nature will always surprise us, and that man can make a difference in our world. Every time I visit the Florida Keys and drive past that Whaling Wall mural, I remember the hawksbill green sea turtle and the important lessons it taught me.

*Wyland*

# More Chicken Soup?

Many of the stories and poems you have read in this book were submitted by readers like you who had read earlier *Chicken Soup for the Soul* books. We publish at least five or six *Chicken Soup for the Soul* books every year. We invite you to contribute a story to one of these future volumes.

Stories may be up to 1,200 words and must uplift or inspire. You may submit an original piece, something you have read or your favorite quotation on your refrigerator door.

To obtain a copy of our submission guidelines and a listing of upcoming *Chicken Soup* books, please write, fax or check our Web site.

Please send your submissions to:

Chicken Soup for the Soul
P.O. Box 30880
Santa Barbara, CA 93130
fax: 805-563-2945
Web site: *www.chickensoup.com*

Just send a copy of your stories and other pieces to the above address.

We will be sure that both you and the author are credited for your submission.

For information about speaking engagements, other books, audiotapes, workshops and training programs, please contact any of our authors directly.

# The Wyland Foundation and Wyland Ocean Challenge

A portion of all proceeds from *Chicken Soup for the Ocean Lover's Soul* will go to the Wyland Foundation, which has partnered with the Scripps Institution of Oceanography at the University of California, San Diego, to create the Wyland Ocean Challenge "Clean Water for the 21st Century"—a free, nationwide marine life art and science educational program for every school in the nation. This program is designed to teach children everywhere about the importance of our marine resources. Your purchase of this book will help make this program a great success.

## Exploring Science Through Art and Imagination

Art is the linchpin that engages interest in science and conservation and fires the imagination, particularly among young students, who will inherit many of the problems we face today. The Wyland Ocean Challenge is the first interdisciplinary art and science educational program for grades K–6 that addresses these issues. The program integrates easily into primary school science units through:

### • Free Downloadable Teacher's Activities

Activities are divided into two grade categories: K–3, 4–6. Three thematic areas are covered to enhance the student's understanding of adaptations, water cycles, and environmental stewardship and conservation. All activities are designed to support National Science and Art Standards.

### • Live Learning Events

A Wyland-designed "Underwater Village" will tour seventeen cities throughout the United States, Canada and Mexico in fall 2003. The tour will supplement the activities of the curriculum.

## • Nationwide Art Contest

An art contest promoting self-expression and science research will take place in late 2003.

The Wyland Foundation is a 501(c)(3) nonprofit organization that inspires people to care more about our oceans and the marine life within. Founded in 1993, the foundation encourages involvement in ocean conservation through classroom education programs, art and scientific research scholarships, and life-size art in public places. Generous monetary and service donations from local, national and individual sponsors make these programs possible.

The origins of the Wyland Foundation begin with the work of artist Wyland, who is recognized by political leaders, scientists, scholars, teachers and environmentalists around the world for his care and concern for our ocean planet.

For more information about the Wyland Foundation or Wyland Ocean Challenge:

Wyland Foundation
P. O. Box 1839
Laguna Beach, CA 926561
phone: 949-497-7979
fax: 949-497-7991
Web sites: *www.wylandfoundation.org*
and *www.wylandoceanchallenge.org*

# Who Is Jack Canfield?

Jack Canfield is one of America's leading experts in the development of human potential and personal effectiveness. He is both a dynamic, entertaining speaker and a highly sought-after trainer. Jack has a wonderful ability to inform and inspire audiences toward increased levels of self-esteem and peak performance.

He is the author and narrator of several bestselling audio- and videocassette programs, including *Self-Esteem and Peak Performance, How to Build High Self-Esteem, Self-Esteem in the Classroom* and *Chicken Soup for the Soul—Live*. He is regularly seen on television shows such as *Good Morning America, 20/20* and *NBC Nightly News*. Jack has co-authored numerous books, including the *Chicken Soup for the Soul* series, *Dare to Win* and *The Aladdin Factor* (all with Mark Victor Hansen), *100 Ways to Build Self-Concept in the Classroom* (with Harold C. Wells), *Heart at Work* (with Jacqueline Miller) and *The Power of Focus* (with Les Hewitt and Mark Victor Hansen).

Jack is a regularly featured speaker for professional associations, school districts, government agencies, churches, hospitals, sales organizations and corporations. His clients have included the American Dental Association, the American Management Association, AT&T, Campbell's Soup, Clairol, Domino's Pizza, GE, ITT, Hartford Insurance, Johnson & Johnson, the Million Dollar Roundtable, NCR, New England Telephone, Re/Max, Scott Paper, TRW and Virgin Records. Jack is also on the faculty of Income Builders International, a school for entrepreneurs.

Jack conducts an annual eight-day Training of Trainers program in the areas of self-esteem and peak performance. It attracts educators, counselors, parenting trainers, corporate trainers, professional speakers, ministers and others interested in developing their speaking and seminar-leading skills.

For further information about Jack's books, tapes and training programs, or to schedule him for a presentation, please contact:

Self-Esteem Seminars
P.O. Box 30880
Santa Barbara, CA 93130
phone: 805-563-2935 • fax: 805-563-2945
Web site: *www.chickensoup.com*

# Who Is Mark Victor Hansen?

Mark Victor Hansen is a professional speaker who, in the last twenty years, has made over four thousand presentations to more than 2 million people in thirty-three countries. His presentations cover sales excellence and strategies; personal empowerment and development; and how to triple your income and double your time off.

Mark has spent a lifetime dedicated to his mission of making a profound and positive difference in people's lives. Throughout his career, he has inspired hundreds of thousands of people to create a more powerful and purposeful future for themselves while stimulating the sale of billions of dollars worth of goods and services.

Mark is a prolific writer and has authored *Future Diary, How to Achieve Total Prosperity* and *The Miracle of Tithing*. He is the coauthor of the *Chicken Soup for the Soul* series, *Dare to Win* and *The Aladdin Factor* (all with Jack Canfield) and *The Master Motivator* (with Joe Batten).

Mark has also produced a complete library of personal empowerment audio- and videocassette programs that have enabled his listeners to recognize and better use their innate abilities in their business and personal lives. His message has made him a popular television and radio personality with appearances on ABC, NBC, CBS, HBO, PBS, QVC and CNN.

He has also appeared on the cover of numerous magazines, including *Success, Entrepreneur* and *Changes*.

Mark is a big man with a heart and a spirit to match—an inspiration to all who seek to better themselves.

For further information about Mark, please contact:

Mark Victor Hansen & Associates
P.O. Box 7665
Newport Beach, CA 92658
phone: 949-759-9304 or 800-433-2314
fax: 949-722-6912
Web site: *www.chickensoup.com*

# Who Is Wyland?

Considered the most influential marine artist of our time, the work of this celebrated painter, sculptor, writer, underwater photographer and muralist is now seen by an estimated one billion people throughout the world every year. Since 1981, he has painted more than ninety monumental marine-life murals, including "Ocean Planet," which was named the largest mural in the world in 1992 by the *Guinness Book of World Records*. Honored in 1998 with the Underwater Society of America's prestigious NOGI Award, he is now listed in that organization's Diving Hall of Fame. He is also founder of the Wyland Foundation, a nonprofit organization dedicated to the preservation of the world's oceans.

Wyland is committed to bridging the worlds of marine science and art—a philosophy hailed by world-renowned ocean scientists such as Dr. Robert Ballard, Dr. Sylvia A. Earle and Dr. Roger Payne. He firmly believes that "if people see the beauty in nature, they will work to preserve it before it's too late."

In 1998, the United Nations honored Wyland by using his art as part of its International Year of the Ocean environmental awareness campaign. Listed among "Who's Who in American Art," the art of Wyland is found today in museums, galleries, on public walls, and in many public and private collections throughout the world.

Wyland can be contacted at:

Wyland Worldwide, LLC.
5 Columbia
Aliso Viejo, CA 92656
phone: 949-643-7070
Web sites: *www.wyland.com* and *www.wylandfoundation.org*

# Who Is Steve Creech?

Steve Creech is a former newspaper reporter who currently serves as publicist for marine-life artist Wyland and the Wyland Foundation. His articles have appeared in such newspapers as *The Orange County Register, Pasadena Star News* and *Anaheim Bulletin,* and magazines such as *Skin Diver, Sport Diver, React for Kids* and *Elan.* He is an active participant in the prestigious Squaw Valley Community of Writers Summer Fiction Workshops in Squaw Valley, California, a children's book author and is currently working on a book of short fiction stories. An avid ocean lover, he has resumed surfing after a twenty-year absence from the sport—and has yet to figure out which foot goes ahead of the other.

For further information about Steve, please write:

Steve Creech
c/o Wyland Worldwide
5 Columbia
Aliso Viejo, CA 92656
phone: 949-643-7070

# Contributors

Several of the stories in this book were taken from previously published sources, such as books, magazines and newspapers. These
sources are acknowledged in the permissions section. If you would
like to contact any of the contributors for information about their
writing or would like to invite them to speak in your community, look
for their contact information included in their biography.

The remainder of the stories were submitted by readers of our previous *Chicken Soup for the Soul* books who responded to our requests
for stories. We have also included information about them.

**Gaie Alling, M.S.,** is the cofounder, CEO and president of Planetary Coral Reef
Foundation. For the past twenty-three years, Ms. Alling has been actively engaged in
marine, environmental and closed systems research and development projects. At
Biosphere 2, she created and operated the largest artificial ecological marine system, a
1 million-gallon mangrove, marsh and ocean coral reef, served as scientific chief for over
sixty research projects and was one of the eight "biospherians" to live inside.

**Jennifer Anderson** lives on the island of Maui where she has recently retired from the
dive industry. During her eighteen-year career, she traveled the world as an underwater
model and led thousands of divers on informative dives, racking up more than twelve
thousand dives. In her leisure time, she now works on manta research and dives from
her kayak for pleasure. Her experiences are penned in a book of stories titled *A Mermaid's
Tale*, soon to be published. She may be reached at *seanymph@Maui.net*.

**Tal Aviezer** and **Jason Cocovinis** are New York City-based writers specializing in
scripts, prose and copy of all kinds. Their work covers a broad range of styles, and they
are always happy to hear of new projects. Contact them at *taviezer@hotmail.com* and
*jcocovinis@hotmail.com*.

**Nancy V. Bennett** is a freelance writer whose passions include history, ghosts and long walks
on country roads. She is a member of the Sooke Scribblers Writing Society and lives on
Vancouver Island with her family. This piece appeared previously in *The Canadian Messenger*.
Her essays have also been aired on CBC radio. Her future plans include publishing a collection of poems on Western outlaws.

**Stephen Byrne** is a freelance outdoor writer with weekly columns in *Nor'east Saltwater*
magazine. You can find his latest column at *www.noreast.com*. He lives in Great Kills and
enjoys the outdoors with his wife Annmarie and sons Stephen and Michael. An active
member of OWAA, you can reach him at *sbyrne@si.rr.com*.

**Anne Carter** is a freelance writer. She and her husband reside on Long Island near the
ocean. Anne began writing to chronicle the events in her life for her grandchildren. She
dedicates this story to her father whose hand she held the first time a wave tickled her
toes. Contact Anne at *carteracdc@webtv.net*.

**Mark Conlin** is a marine wildlife photographer. He holds a degree in marine biology
from University of California Santa Barbara. Mark's hope is that his background in

marine biology and love for the ocean can help illustrate an environment that needs our protection. To see Mark's photography, please visit his Web site at *www.markconlin.com.*

**Clive Cussler** is famous as America's Grandmaster of Adventure. His books are in forty languages in 110 countries and have sold over 130 million copies. A noted shipwreck hunter, he and his NUMA crew have discovered over sixty historic shipwrecks.

The late **Lester David** was a veteran magazine writer and newspaper editor as well as the author of numerous biographies of well-known figures in politics and the arts.

**Dayle Ann Dodds** has published eleven books, newspaper articles, poems and magazine stories for children. Her first picture book, *Wheel Away!* was number one on the *San Francisco Chronicle's* bestseller list. Dayle just completed another novel and her first full-length screenplay.

**Dr. Sylvia A. Earle** is an oceanographer, explorer, author, lecturer, consultant, National Geographic Explorer-in-Residence, executive director of Global Marine Programs for Conservation International, program director for the Harte Research Institute, chairman of Deep Ocean Exploration and Research, and former chief scientist of the National Oceanic and Atmospheric Administration.

Acclaimed as "The Goodness-Maker," **Joycebelle Edelbrock** is the author and illustrator of ten kids' e-books, including several underwater stories for kids and those about diving with Jacques Cousteau. Her work appears in a wide range of forums, from *National Geographic, International and National Wildlife, Ranger Rick, World* and *Skin Diver* to *Chicken Soup for the Teacher's Soul.* Visit her Web site at *www.joycebelle.com* where you can download a free e-book, *Around the World Underwater with Jacques Cousteau.*

**Linda Schnecker Erb** is Vice-President of Animal Care and Training at Dolphin Research Center (DRC) and is currently writing a book about her many "dolfriends," including Annessa. The not-for-profit DRC brings people and dolphins together for educational encounters and other experiences. Contact Linda at Dolphin Research Center, 58901 Overseas Highway, Grassy Key, FL 33050, or visit *www.dolphins.org.*

**Mike Geers** graduated with honors from the University of Central Florida. He served in the U.S. Navy and Coast Guard. He works at SRI International and is completing his law degree in California. He hopes to write a book on the humanitarian aspects of psychic phenomena in search and rescue. Contact him at *MikeGeers@hotmail.com.*

**Florian Graner** is a marine biologist and freelance photographer. He specializes in underwater cinematography and photography. He has worked as a cameraman in projects for the BBC such as "The Blue Planet," "Extreme Animals" and "Wildlife on One." Florian can be reached through his Web site at *www.sealife-productions.com.*

**Martha Gusukuma-Donnenfield** received her B.A. and teaching credentials from California State University, Long Beach. She has been teaching in Long Beach for over twenty-two years. Martha loves taking Stephen, her husband, and two children, home to Hawaii to experience what island life is all about.

**Jack Hanna** is the host of *Animal Adventures,* a weekly TV show featuring wildlife, which is broadcast in more than sixty-five countries internationally. He is also a regular guest on such popular shows as ABC's *Good Morning America,* CNN's *Larry King Live* and CBS's *Late Show with David Letterman.* Jack's love for animals and nature has also spawned several books, including *Monkeys on the Interstate, Jungle Jack Hanna's Safari Adventure, What Zookeepers Do* and *The Ultimate Guide to Pets.*

**Eve Eschner Hogan** is an author, speaker and co-owner of Makena Coast Dive Charters on Maui. She is also a wedding officiant, specializing in underwater and boat weddings. For information on her workshops, books or weddings, see *www.HeartPath.com* or e-mail *Eve@HeartPath.com*. For Maui Scuba Diving, see *www.MauiUnderwater.com* or call 800-833-6483.

**Warren Iliff** is the President-Emeritus of the Aquarium of the Pacific and oversaw its opening in 1998. Prior to that, he was the director of zoos in Phoenix, Dallas and Portland, Oregon. He is a graduate of Harvard and a former Marine Corps helicopter pilot. Please reach him at *wiliff@ibaop.org*.

**Jamie Kageleiry** wrote this story for *Yankee Magazine,* which has been "The Magazine of New England Living" for sixty-eight years. They are located on Main Street, Dublin, NH 03444. Phone: 603-563-8111. Web site: *www.yankeemagazine.com*.

**Jim Kravets** says, "There's just something about the ocean." When pressed for elaboration, he managed, "You know, the fish, the . . . saltiness. I'm just so drawn to oceans. I'm going to the Aegean for my honeymoon." When asked if the Aegean isn't technically a sea and not an ocean, he said, "I really don't know. The travel agent made the bookings." Jim lives and writes in northern California. Contact him at *jimk@backroads.com*.

**Phil Lansing** has worked on ranches, in the forest and on fishing boats. He has traveled by canoe through Arctic Canada and guided canoe trips down the wild Owyhee River in Southwest Idaho. He was educated at Oxford University and works as an economist consulting in natural resource issues. He is based in Idaho with his wife, two children and bird dog.

**Nan Lincoln** continues to live on Mount Desert Island off the coast of Maine where she is the arts editor and a feature writer for the *Bar Harbor Times*. She also continues to call out "Sessileeeee!" whenever she's on or near the sea. Sometimes she gets an answer.

**Mike Lipstock's** work has appeared in close to two hundred literary magazines, newspapers and anthologies. He has received three Pushcart Prize nominations and a multitude of first prizes in various publications. He has also been published in four previous *Chicken Soup for the Soul* books.

**Jennifer Lowry** was born in New Orleans, Louisiana. She is the older sister of Shannon and Jason. She attends the University of New Orleans, where she is studying business, with her husband Donald, who studies engineering. This is her first opportunity to have something published in memory of her sister.

**Janet Matthews** is a writer, editor, professional speaker and coauthor of the bestselling *Chicken Soup for the Canadian Soul*. With Daniel Keenan, she is working on a book-sized version of "The Navy's Baby," an amazing story appearing in *Chicken Soup for the Parent's Soul,* which she helped produce and edit. To schedule Janet for an interview or speaking engagement, contact her at 905-881-8995, ext. 28, or *janet@canadiansoul.com,* or go to *www.canadiansoul.com*.

**Paula McDonald** has sold over a million copies of her books on relationships and has won numerous awards worldwide as a columnist, inspirational feature writer and photojournalist. She lives on the beach in Rosarito, Mexico, and writes to the sound of the waves. She can be contacted in the United States by writing PMB 724, 416 W. San Ysidro Blvd., Ste. L, San Ysidro, CA 92173-2443 or by e-mailing *eieiho@msn.com*.

**Walker Meade** began to write stories at the age of fourteen. When he was twenty-one, one of his pieces was published by *Colliers* magazine. He then wrote short fiction for the *Saturday Evening Post, Good Housekeeping* and *Gentleman's Quarterly*, among others. He turned to writing nonfiction for magazines such as *Cosmopolitan, Reader's Digest* and *Redbook*. Later he became the managing editor of *Cosmopolitan* and then the managing editor of *Reader's Digest* Condensed Book Club. His last position in publishing was as president and editor-in-chief of Avon Books. Today he is retired and concentrates on writing longer fiction. Upstart Press published his first novel, *Unspeakable Acts*, in August 2001. It has received exciting critical acclaim and can be ordered from *Amazon.com*. He has just finished his second novel.

**Jan Meek** has packed so much into her fifty-four years that her life reads like the plot of a book, from working in the film business with well-known stars, to living and working in Saudi Arabia, to being elected mayor of her hometown, to learning Chinese while backpacking around China, to her *Guiness Book of World Records* Atlantic rowing record. Now a professional speaker, she's authored the book, *101 Atlantic Nights*, the full version of her Atlantic crossing with her son, Daniel. She also has a daughter, Becky. Jan lives in Chipping Norton, England, and can be contacted at *JaniceMeek@aol.com*.

**Warren Miller** started his lifelong search for the free ski-lift ticket in 1946. Since then he has produced over five hundred sports films, written nine books and raised three children. He writes a weekly newspaper column, monthly magazine articles and is working on his autobiography. He can be reached at *Warren@WarrenMiller.net*.

**Joe Moran** received a bachelor of science in marine biology from the College of Charleston (S.C.) in 1984. He currently is working in Washington, D.C., still in the field of marine science. He is a husband and a dad, an avid Scouter, and still wonders what that whale was thinking.

**Deborah Morris** is the author of fifteen books, including the *Real Kids Real Adventures* book series (adapted as an Emmy-nominated television series on the Discovery Channel), and *Teens 911: Snowbound*, a new real-life survival series. Deborah lives in Texas with her husband, her Harley, and her own "real kids." Visit the Web site *www.realkids.com*.

**Abby Murray** received her bachelor's degree in psychology from the University of Illinois-Urbana and her master's degree in counselor education from North Carolina State University. Married to Jim, they are the proud parents of a beautiful little girl named Ellen and are expecting their second child. Abby is the volunteer manager at the John G. Shedd Aquarium in Chicago where she manages over 600 volunteers. She can be reached at *amurray@sheddaquarium.org* or 312-692-3310.

**Bruce Nash** of Studio City, California, produces television shows for various networks and cable channels.

**Tiffany Pope** is an aspiring writer from Norfolk, Virginia. She graduated from high school in 2001 and is currently studying for an associate degree in liberal arts. After that she plans to transfer to a four-year college and major in journalism.

**Maurice Ricketts** is a navy veteran of World War II and a country boy from Wyoming. His detailed memoir, *As It Was*, depicts life as an orphan chore boy on a sheep ranch and a destroyer sailor on the high seas in wartime.

**Gary Riedel** enjoys creating. After his onstage work at the Aquarium, he became a background actor in Hollywood. His first novel, *Seasons of the Pearl*, is available on *Amazon.com*. He describes it as a comedy of war seen from inside a Saigon bistro in wartime Vietnam. Contact Gary at *GoodGate@msn.com*.

**Jon L. Rishi** received his bachelor of arts degree from Chaminade University, Honolulu, in 1986. He grew up in Hawaii and currently resides in Orange County, California, where he is a healthcare administrator. Jon enjoys travel, recreational running, skiing and water sports. He considers literature and creative writing a lifelong passion. Please reach him at *JLRishi@aol.com*.

**Danette Rivera** is a Southern California-based writer who lives with her two "smart, gorgeous" daughters Maya and Mina, a "hot husband" named Julio, and a "fat, lazy cat" named Puffy. A small business owner, she has been a past participant in the prestigious Squaw Valley Community of Writers Summer Workshops and was recently published in *Riviera Magazine*. When she has spare time, she spends it romping with her girls, writing short fiction and sports essays, and salsa dancing.

**Nicole-René Rivette** is a college student who lives in Midland, Michigan, with her parents and two dogs. Horseback riding has been a lifelong love, and she hopes to try out for the U.S. Equestrian Team in their Developing Riders category. Volunteer work, vegetarian cooking, kayaking and writing stories round out her busy schedule.

**Harley Schwadron's** cartoons appear in such diverse publications as *Barron's, Wall Street Journal, Reader's Digest, Harvard Business Review, Good Housekeeping* and many others. He has worked as a newspaper reporter, college alumni magazine editor and university public-relations editor. After doing cartoons on evenings and weekends, he went full-time in 1984 and is still going strong. He can be reached at P.O. Box 1347, Ann Arbor, MI 48106 or by phone/fax at 734-426-8433.

**Maris Sidenstecker** founded Save The Whales (STW) at the age of fourteen. Maris, a marine biologist, continues to lead STW and focuses on educating children and adults about marine mammals and the fragile ocean environment. STW provides school outreach, educational materials and adopt-a-whale kits. She can be reached at 831-899-9957 or visit *www.savethewhales.org*.

**Leslie Smith** spent twenty years on Kodiak Island where she captained her own boat, fishing commercially for salmon and halibut. Her two children were born there. She currently lives in Idaho during the school year and returns to Alaska with her teenage daughters in the summers to gillnet for salmon, pick berries and play croquet on the beach.

**Roxayne Spruance** received bachelor degrees in zoology and physical anthropology at the University of California, Davis. She has been a volunteer with the Sea Otter Research and Conservation team at the Monterey Bay Aquarium since 1995 and is on the board of the Friends of the Sea Otter, a nonprofit group dedicated to their protection. Please reach her at *spruancer@pebblebeach.com*.

Michelle Staedler received a bachelor's degree in environmental studies from the University of California, Santa Cruz. She has been working with sea otters in the Monterey area for over fifteen years as the research coordinator for the Monterey Bay Aquarium's Sea Otter Research and Conservation Program. In addition to her work with sea otters, Michelle enjoys introducing her young son to new adventures, collecting marbles and raising lop-eared rabbits. Please reach her at *mstaedler@mbayaq.org.*

Maggie Stapp-Hempen, a Laguna Beach, California, resident, is the mother of two grown children, daughter Malea and son Aaron. She has been active in many community organizations, including Laguna Art Museum and the local Business Development Council. Maggie is happily and recently married to Tony and enjoys spending time with his two children David and Elise.

Matt Walker is a native East Coaster currently held hostage in California as Senior Editor of *Surfing Magazine.* A lifelong devotee to both the ocean and the written word, he plans on using his *Chicken Soup* paycheck to buy yet another surboard, perhaps for his son McRae—if he's lucky.

Nathan S. Woods received his bachelor of arts degree from Loyola University in 1999. He is a hip-hop artist, poet and writer in New Orleans. He enjoys walking, people-watching, video games and good conversation. He plans to write a book of poetry. Please reach him at *silvertonguedpoet@yahoo.com.*

Jennifer Zambri-Dickerson, a New Jersey native, is a graduate of the University of Delaware with a bachelor's degree in animal science. Jennifer currently lives in Dover, Delaware, with her husband and two children. She is working on her first novel. Jennifer can be reached at *zambrij@comcast.net.*

Liz Zuercher moved from Chicago to California after earning her English degree from DePauw University. She put writing on hold to raise two sons and operate a graphic-arts business with her husband. Recently, she returned to studying writing, authoring short stories and essays, as well as editing colleagues' work.

Allan Zullo, of Fairview, North Carolina, is the author of more than seventy nonfiction books on a variety of topics.

*Sea Dog.* Reprinted by permission of Jon L. Rishi. ©2002 Jon L. Rishi.

*What Do You See?* Reprinted by permission of Gary Riedel. ©2001 Gary Riedel.

*A Lesson from the Sea.* Reprinted by permission of Walker Meade. ©2002 Walker Meade.

*The Day at the Beach.* Reprinted by permission of Arthur Gordon. ©1999 Arthur Gordon.

*The Sea and the Wind That Blows* by E. B. White. Reprinted by permission of the E. B. White Estate. Originally published in the *Ford Times,* Vol. 56, Issue June 1963, pp. 2–6.

*The Driftwood Queen.* Reprinted by permission of Anne Carter. ©2002 Anne Carter.

*A Sign of Love.* Reprinted by permission of Warren Iliff. ©2002 Warren Iliff.

*Sand Castles.* Excerpted from *And the Angels Were Silent.* ©1992 by Max Lucado. Used by permission of Multnomah Publishers, Inc.

*Sea of Curiosity* and *The Specialist.* Reprinted by permission of Sylvia A. Earle. ©1996 Sylvia A. Earle. From chapter 2 of *Sea Change: A Message of the Oceans.* ©1996.

*Who's Watching Who?* Reprinted by permission of Joe Moran. ©2002 Joe Moran.

*The Jonah Factor.* Reprinted by permission of Mark Conlin. ©1998 Mark Conlin. Appeared in production notes of PBS program, "Secrets of the Ocean Realm" at *www.pbs.org/oceanrealm/producers/index.html.*

*Close Encounter of the Squid Kind.* Reprinted by permission of Mark Conlin. ©1998 Mark Conlin. Appeared in production notes of PBS program, "Secrets of the Ocean Realm" at *www.pbs.org/oceanrealm/producers/index.html.*

*Finding His Way Home.* Reprinted by permission of Clive Cussler. ©1993 Clive Cussler.

*Eyes in the Dark.* Excerpted from *Kon-Tiki* by Thor Heyerdahl. ©GYLDENDAL NORSK FORLAG AS. 1948; pp. 117–119.

*Fred's Big Adventure.* Reprinted by permission of Mark Conlin. ©1998 Mark Conlin. Appeared in production notes of PBS program, "Secrets of the Ocean Realm" at *www.pbs.org/oceanrealm/producers/index.html.*

*Last One Standing.* Reprinted by permission of Phil Lansing. ©2001 Phil Lansing.

*Geriatric Genocide.* Reprinted by permission of Warren Miller. ©1994 Warren Miller.

*A Shot at the Title.* Reprinted by permission of Jim Kravets. ©2002 Jim Kravets.

*Father Time.* Reprinted by permission of Matt Walker. ©2001 Matt Walker.

*Two Battleships.* Reprinted by permission of Maurice Ricketts. ©2003 Maurice Ricketts.